Workshop on Automated Event Extraction of Socio-political Events from News (AESPEN2020)

Marseille, France
11 – 16 May 2020

Editors:

Ali Hurriyetoglu
Erdem Yoruk
Hristo Tanev
Vanni Zavarella

ISBN: 978-1-7138-1252-4

Printed from e-media with permission by:

Curran Associates, Inc.
57 Morehouse Lane
Red Hook, NY 12571

Some format issues inherent in the e-media version may also appear in this print version.

Association for Computational Linguistics
209 N. Eighth Street
Stroudsburg, Pennsylvania 18360

Phone: 1-570-476-8006
Fax: 1-570-476-0860

acl@aclweb.org

Additional copies of this publication are available from:

Curran Associates, Inc.
57 Morehouse Lane
Red Hook, NY 12571 USA
Phone: 845-758-0400
Fax: 845-758-2633
Email: curran@proceedings.com
Web: www.proceedings.com

LREC 2020 Workshop
Language Resources and Evaluation Conference
11–16 May 2020

Workshop on Automated Event Extraction of Socio-political Events from News (AESPEN2020)

PROCEEDINGS

Editors:
Ali Hürriyetoğlu (Koc University)
Erdem Yörük (Koc University and University of Oxford)
Hristo Tanev (European Commission Joint Research Center)
Vanni Zavarella (European Commission Joint Research Center)

Proceedings of the LREC 2020 Workshop on Automated Event Extraction of Socio-political Events from News (AESPEN2020)

Edited by: Ali Hürriyetoğlu, Erdem Yörük, Hristo Tanev, and Vanni Zavarella

For more information:
European Language Resources Association (ELRA)
9 rue des Cordelières
75013, Paris
France
http://www.elra.info
Email: lrec@elda.org

Introduction

This year we've accepted for publication nine papers which look at event detection from different points of view.

Nine papers were regular paper submissions and one was a shared task participation report. The shared task report and seven of the regular papers were accepted on the basis of reviews, which were five per paper, performed by the program committee members.

The accepted regular papers can be grouped as i) evaluation of state-of-the-art machine learning approaches by Buyukoz et al., Olsson et al., and Piskorski, and Jacquet, ii) introduction of a new data set by Radford, iii) projects of event information collection by Osorio et al. and Papanikolaou and Papageorgiou, and iv) forecasting of political conflict by Halkia et al.

The evaluation of Buyukoz et al. and Olsson et al. show that state-of-the-art deep learning models such as BERT and ELMo (Peters et al., 2018) yield consistently higher performance than traditional ML methods such as support vector machines (SVM) on conflict and protest event data respectively. Piskorski and Jacquet have found that TF-IDFweighted character n-gram based SVM model performs better than an SVM model that facilitates pre-trained em-beddings such as GLOVE (Pennington et al., 2014), BERT, and FASTTEXT (Mikolov et al., 2018) in most of the experiments on conflict data. Radford introduces the dataset Headlines of War for cross-document coreference resolution for the news headlines.The dataset consists of positive samples from Militarized Interstate Disputes dataset and negative samples from NewYork Times. The description of this invaluable resource accompanied with a detailed discussion of its utility and caveats. Osorio et al. introduce Hadath that is a supervised protocol for event information collection from Arabic sources. The utility of Hadath was demonstrated in processing news reported between 2012 and 2012 in Afghanistan. In the scope of the other event information collection study, Papanikolaou and Papageorgiou processed two news sourcesi in Greek from Greece to create a database of protest events for the period between 1996 and 2014. Osorio et. al. and Pa-panikolaou and Papageorgiou utilized fully automatic toolsthat integrates supervised machine learning and rule based methodologies at various degrees. Finally, Halkia et al. presents a material conflict forecastingstudy that facilitates the available event databases GDELT and ICEWS. Their results demonstrate that it is possible to correctly predict social upheaval using the methodology they propose, which utilizes Long-Short Term Memory(LSTM) (Hochreiter and Schmidhuber, 1997).We have received expression of interest from 12 research teams, of which 6 teams signed the application form and received the data. Two of these teams sent their predictions on the test data. Finally, only Ors et al. submitted a paper about their work. This team reported their work as consisting of three steps. First, they use a transformer based model,which is ALBERT (Lan et al., 2020), to predict whether apair of sentences refer to the same event or not. Later, they use these predictions as the initial scores and recalculate their scores by considering the relation of sentences in a pair with respect to other sentences. As the last step, final scores between these sentences are used to construct the clusters,starting with the pairs with the highest scores.

The variety of the submitted papers show that we could bring the ML, NLP, and social and political science communities together. Although the breadth of the topics were limited, the technical depth and timeliness of the contributions show that the workshop contribute to the discipline of automatic extraction of socio-political events. The papers about processing Arabic and Greek sources are significant contributions to the understanding of how should we handle languages other than English. Finally, the shared task ESCI demonstrated the prevalence of the event coreferences, some baselines for handling them, and a state-of-the-art system that is able to tackle this task.

Organizers:

Ali Hürriyetoğlu (Koc University)
Erdem Yörük (Koc University and University of Oxford)
Hristo Tanev (European Commission – Joint Research Center)
Vanni Zavarella (European Commission – Joint Research Center)

Program Committee:

Svetla Boycheva (Institute of Information and Communication Technologies, Bulgarian Academy of Sciences)
Fırat Duruşan (Koc University)
Theresa Gessler (University of Zürich)
Christian Göbel (University of Vienna)
Burak Gürel (Koc University)
Matina Halkia (European Commission – Joint Research Center)
Sophia Hunger (European University Institute)
J. Craig Jenkins (The Ohio State University)
Liron Lavi (UCLA Y&S Nazarian Center for Israel Studies)
Jasmine Lorenzini (University of Geneva)
Bernardo Magnini (Fondazione Bruno Kessler (FBK))
Osman Mutlu (Koc University)
Nelleke Oostdijk (Radboud University)
Arzucan Özgür (Boğaziçi University)
Jakub Piskorski (Polish Academy of Sciences)
Lidia Pivovarova (University of Helsinki)
Benjamin J. Radford (UNC Charlotte)
Clionadh Raleigh (University of Sussex)
Ali Safaya (Koc University)
Parang Saraf (Virginia Tech)
Philip Schrodt (Parus Analytical Systems)
Manuela Speranza (Fondazione Bruno Kessler, Trento)
Çağrı Yoltar (Koc University)
Aline Villavicencio (The University of Sheffield)
Kalliopi Zervanou (Eindhoven University of Technology)

Invited Speakers:

Clionadh Raleigh, University of Sussex
Philip Schrodt (Parus Analytical Systems)

Table of Contents

Workshop Program

Proceedings of AESPEN 2020, pages 1–6
Language Resources and Evaluation Conference (LREC 2020), Marseille, 11–16 May 2020

Automated Extraction of Socio-political Events from News (AESPEN): Workshop and Shared Task Report

Ali Hürriyetoğlu[*], Vanni Zavarella[†], Hristo Tanev[†], Erdem Yörük[*], Ali Safaya[*], Osman Mutlu[*]
[*]Koç University,
Rumelifeneri Yolu 34450, Sarıyer, İstanbul/Turkey
{ahurriyetoglu, eryoruk, asafaya19, omutlu}@ku.edu.tr

[†]European Commission Joint Research Centre
Via E. Fermi, 2749, 21027 Ispra VA, Italy
{vanni.zavarella, hristo.tanev}@ec.europa.eu

Abstract

We describe our effort on automated extraction of socio-political events from news in the scope of a workshop and a shared task we organized at Language Resources and Evaluation Conference (LREC 2020). We believe the event extraction studies in computational linguistics and social and political sciences should further support each other in order to enable large scale socio-political event information collection across sources, countries, and languages. The event consists of regular research papers and a shared task, which is about event sentence coreference identification (ESCI), tracks. All submissions were reviewed by five members of the program committee. The workshop attracted research papers related to evaluation of machine learning methodologies, language resources, material conflict forecasting, and a shared task participation report in the scope of socio-political event information collection. It has shown us the volume and variety of both the data sources and event information collection approaches related to socio-political events and the need to fill the gap between automated text processing techniques and requirements of social and political sciences.

Keywords: socio-political events, information extraction, event extraction, machine learning, natural language processing, computational linguistics, social sciences, political sciences

1. Introduction

Automatic construction of socio-political event databases has long been a challenge for the natural language processing (NLP) and social and political science communities in terms of algorithmic approaches and language resources required to develop automated tools (Chenoweth and Lewis, 2013; Weidmann and Rød, 2019; Raleigh et al., 2010). At the same time, social and political scientists have been working on creating socio-political event databases for decades using manual (Yoruk, 2012), semi-automatic (Nardulli et al., 2015), and automatic approaches (Leetaru and Schrodt, 2013; Boschee et al., 2013; Schrodt et al., 2014; Sönmez et al., 2016). However, the results yielded by these approaches to date are either not of sufficient quality or require tremendous effort to be replicated on new data (Wang et al., 2016; Ward et al., 2013; Ettinger et al., 2017). On the one hand, manual or semi-automatic methods require high-quality human effort; on the other hand, state-of-the-art automated event detection systems are not accurate enough for their output to be used directly without human moderation.

The NLP community has achieved some consensus on the treatment of events both in terms of task definition and appropriate techniques for their detection (Pustejovsky et al., 2005; Doddington et al., 2004; Song et al., 2015; Getman et al., 2018). However, in order to be useful, these formalisms and related systems need to be adjusted or extended for each type of event in relation to certain use cases. The social and political scientists spend a similar effort for formalising event types such as (CAMEO) (Gerner et al., 2002) and implement the aforementioned systems that vary from rule-based to fully automatic approaches. Unfortunately, any new project in this line still finds itself making design decisions such as using only the heading sentences in a news article or not considering coreference information (Boschee et al., 2013) without being able to quantify their effect. Therefore, we think these communities should investigate ways of supporting each other in order to reach a consensus and enable any prospective event information collection project as robustly and predictably as possible.

Given the aforementioned limitations, there is an increasing tendency to rely on machine learning (ML) and NLP methods to deal better with the vast amount and variety of data to be processed. Consequently, we thought it was time to held a workshop on Automated Extraction of Socio-political Events from News (AESPEN)[1] at Language Resources and Evaluation Conference (LREC 2020).[2] The purpose of this workshop was to inspire the emergence of innovative technological and scientific solutions in the field of event detection and event metadata extraction from news, as well as the development of evaluation metrics for socio-political event recognition. Moreover, the workshop aimed at triggering a deeper understanding of the usability of socio-political event datasets.

We organized a shared task as a continuation of the Conference and Labs of the Evaluation Forum (CLEF 2019) task ProtestNews (Hürriyetoğlu et al., 2019a; Hürriyetoğlu et al., 2019b), which was on cross-context document clas-

[1] `https://emw.ku.edu.tr/aespen-2020/`, accessed on April 18, 2020.

[2] `https://lrec2020.lrec-conf.org/`, accessed on April 18, 2020.

sification, event sentence detection, and event extraction pertaining to protest events. We aimed at establishing a benchmark for the event sentence coreference identification (ESCI) sub-task within the scope of the AESPEN workshop. The scope of this shared task was on clustering given event related sentences so that each cluster consists of sentences about the same event.

We provide details of our motivation in Section 2. Then, we introduce the ESCI shared task in Section 3. Finally, we briefly describe the accepted papers and the shared task results in Section 4. We conclude this report in section 5.

2. Motivation

Automating political event collection requires the availability of gold-standard corpora that can be used for system development and evaluation. Moreover, automated tool performances need to be reproducible and comparable. Although a tremendous effort is being spent on creating socio-political event databases such as ACLED (Raleigh et al., 2010), the Global Database of Events, Language, and Tone (GDELT) (Leetaru and Schrodt, 2013), the Mass Mobilization on Autocracies Database (MMAD) (Weidmann and Rød, 2019), the Integrated Crisis Early Warning System (ICEWS) (Boschee et al., 2013), and the Protest Dataset 30 European countries (PolDem) (Kriesi et al., 2019) we believe there is still a lot of room for improvement and harmonisation of the event schemas and tasks. This limitation causes the definition of the events and automated event information collection tool performances to be restricted to single projects. Consequently, the lack of comparable and reproducible settings hinders progress on this task.

We invited contributions from researchers in NLP, ML and Artificial Intelligence (AI) involved in automated event data collection, as well as researchers in social and political sciences, conflict analysis and peace studies, who make use of this kind of data for their analytical work. Our goal was to enable the emergence of innovative NLP and information extraction (IE) solutions that can deal with the current stream of information, manage the risks of information overload, identify different sources and perspectives, and provide unitary and intelligible representations of the larger and long-term storylines behind news articles.

Our workshop provided a venue for discussing the creation and facilitation of language resources in the social and political sciences domain. Social and political scientists were interested in reporting and discussing the automated tools and comparing traditional coding approaches with automated tools. Computational linguistics and machine learning practitioners and researchers benefited from being challenged by real-world use cases, in terms of event data extraction, representation and aggregation.

We invited work on all aspects of automated coding of socio-political events from monolingual or multilingual news sources. This includes (but is not limited to) the following topics: event metadata extraction, source bias mitigation, event data schema and representation, event information duplication detection, extracting events beyond a sentence in a document, training data collection and annotation processes, event coreference (in- and cross-document), sub-event and event subset relations, event dataset evaluation and validity metrics, event datasets quality assessments, defining, populating and facilitating event ontologies, automated tools for relevant subtasks, understanding the limits that are introduced by copyright rules and ethical concerns and ethical design.

3. Shared Task

A news article may contain one or more events that are expressed with one or more sentences. Identifying event sentences that are about the same event is necessary in order to collect event information robustly. Therefore, we should develop methods that are able to identify whether a group of sentences are about the same event. Reliable identification of this relation will enable us to determine how many events are reported in a news article as well. Moreover, solving this problem has the potential to facilitate cross-document event sentence relation identification in the long term. Therefore, we should develop methods that are able to identify whether a group of event sentences are about the same event. Consequently, we organized the ESCI shared task in the hopes of attracting attention to this problem and possibly provide a benchmark for it.

We examined our gold standard corpus that contains 1,290 events in 712 documents annotated at token level for their event information (Hürriyetoğlu et al., 2019a; Hürriyetoğlu et al., 2019b; Hürriyetoğlu et al., 2020). These documents are the positively labelled instances of random samples and active learning based samples based on these random samples. We have observed that 60% of the news articles contain information about a single event. The remaining documents contain information about multiple events, which sums up to 45% of the total event count. Only 45% of the events are expressed with only a single sentence.

Consequently, we think protest event collection systems should take these phenomena into account and introduce the ESCI shared task. As training data participants of the data challenge received event related sentences and their true clustering in a news article, in which a cluster represents all sentences about an event. This data was extracted from 404 documents. The documents that contain a single event sentence were excluded from this exercise, since there is only one possible clustering in that case. The number of events per document in the training data is 1 for 207 and 2 for 132 documents. The remaining 65 documents contain 3 or more events. The task of the participants was to develop systems that can predict grouping of the given sentences that consists of events on test data, extracted from 100 documents, and that was delivered to them one week before the deadline. The correct grouping of the test set was not shared with the participants. The evaluation metric is Adjusted Rand Index (ARI) as implemented by Scikit-learn (Hubert and Arabie, 1985).[3] We calculated macro and micro versions of this score. The macro version calculates average of the per document scores from all of the documents independent of how many event sentences are there in each document. However, the micro score weights the

[3]`https://scikit-learn.org/stable/modules/generated/sklearn.metrics.adjusted_rand_score.html`, accessed on April 19, 2020.

per document score with the number of the event sentences in a document. We report the F1 score that is calculated similarly as well.

The event type is a protest in the scope of this task. The event we simply refer to as protest events are comprised within the scope of contentious politics. Contentious politics events refers to politically motivated collective action events which lay outside the official mechanisms of political participation associated with formal government institutions of the country in which the said action takes place.[4]

The data is shared with the researchers, who signed an application form that limits the use of the data only for research purposes, as a file that contains lines of JSON objects. Each JSON object contain all event sentences that are identified in a news article and their clustering, which is found in the *event_clusters* field.

A sample JSON object is presented below. The *url* field is provided only as an ID. The numbers in the *sentence_no* correspond to sentences in the *sentences* field in the same order. The *event_clusters* field provides the correct clustering of the event sentences. For instance, below in Listing 1, the first and third sentences are about the same event. But, the second sentence is about a separate event.

Listing 1: Event sentences that are extracted from a document in the order they occur in a sentence.

```
{
  "url": "http://www.newindianexpress.
      com/nation/2009/aug/25/congress-
      demands-advanis-apology-80257",
  "sentences": [
    "Singh had recently blamed Advani
        for coming to Gujarat Chief
        Minister Narendra Modi ' s
        rescue and ensured that he was
        not sacked , in the wake of the
         riots .",
    "On Kandahar plane hijack issue ,
        Singh said Advani was not
        speaking the truth .",
    "Elaborating on the three issues ,
        Singhvi said , The BJP gave
        sermons on Raj Dharma and
        turned a Nelson ' s eye to the
        communal carnage , which became
         a big blot on the fair name of
         the country ."
  ],
  "sentence_no": [4, 6, 14],
  "event_clusters": [[4, 14], [6]]
}
```

We have calculated three baseline scores on the test data. First, we checked score of a dummy predictor that assigns all event sentences to a single cluster all the time, i.e., minimum cluster prediction (MinC). Second, another dummy baseline predicts as each event sentence as being in a separate cluster in a document, i.e., maximum cluster prediction (MaxC). Finally, we used BERT sentence representations (Devlin et al., 2019) to train a multilayer perceptron (MLP) model that i) first evaluates each possible sentence pair in the document, ii) then assign a positive or negative label indicating that this pair of sentences is co-referent, iii) finally using the correlation clustering algorithm (Bansal et al., 2004) we take those labeled pairs and cluster them. [5]

The scores of these methods are provided in Table 1 as *MinC*, *MaxC*, and *MLP*. The slightly low scores obtained from the dummy systems direct us to use the MLP system as the baseline we share with the participants. Note that the strength of the dummy baselines changes according to data distribution in test data.

	ARI		F1	
	Macro	Micro	Macro	Micro
MinC	.5000	.4040	.5000	.4040
MaxC	.1071	.0628	.3476	.3722
MLP	.5077	.4064	.5560	.4840

Table 1: Adjusted Random Index (ARI) and F1 for each baseline system.

4. Submissions

The workshop has attracted nine papers as regular paper submissions and one as a shared task participation report. The shared task report and seven of the regular papers were accepted on the basis of the reviews, which were five per paper, performed by the program committee members.

The accepted regular papers can be grouped as i) evaluation of state-of-the-art machine learning approaches by Büyüköz et al. (2020), Olsson et al. (2020), and Piskorski and Jacquet (2020), ii) introduction of a new data set by Radford (2020), iii) projects of event information collection by Osorio et al. (2020) and Papanikolaou and Papageorgiou1 (2020), and iv) forecasting of political conflict by Halkia et al. (2020).

The evaluation of Büyüköz et al. (2020) and Olsson et al. (2020) show that state-of-the-art deep learning models such as BERT and ELMo (Peters et al., 2018) yield consistently higher performance than traditional ML methods such as support vector machines (SVM) on conflict and protest event data respectively. Piskorski and Jacquet (2020) have found that TF-IDF weighted character n-gram based SVM model performs better than an SVM model that uses pre-trained embeddings such as GLOVE (Pennington et al., 2014), BERT, and FASTTEXT (Mikolov et al., 2018) in most of the experiments on conflict data.

Radford (2020) introduces the dataset *Headlines of War* for cross-document coreference resolution for the news headlines. The dataset consists of positive samples from *Militarized Interstate Disputes* dataset and negative samples

[4] You can find detailed information about how a protest is defined and how event sentences are labelled on our annotation manual, which is on `https://github.com/emerging-welfare/general_info/tree/master/annotation-manuals`.

[5] The code for this system is available on `https://github.com/alisafaya/event-coreference`, accessed on April 21, 2020.

from New York Times.[6] The description of this invaluable resource is accompanied with a detailed discussion of its utility and caveats.

Osorio et al. (2020) introduce Hadath that is a supervised protocol for event information collection from Arabic sources. The utility of Hadath was demonstrated in processing news reported between 2012 and 2012 in Afghanistan. In the scope of the other event information collection study, Papanikolaou and Papageorgioul (2020) processed two news sources in Greek from Greece to create a database of protest events for the period between 1996 and 2014. Osorio et al and Papanikolaou and Papageorgiou utilized fully automatic tools that integrate supervised machine learning and rule based methodologies at various degrees.

Finally, Halkia et al. (2020) presents a material conflict forecasting study that exploits available event databases GDELT and ICEWS. Their results demonstrate that it is possible to correctly predict social upheaval using the methodology they propose, which utilizes Long-Short Term Memory (LSTM) (Hochreiter and Schmidhuber, 1997).

We have received expression of interest from 12 research teams, of which 6 teams signed the application form and received the data. Two of these teams sent their predictions on the test data. The scores of these methods are illustrated in Table 2. Finally, only Örs et al. (2020) submitted a paper about their work. This team reported their work as consisting of three steps. First, they use a transformer based model, which is ALBERT (Lan et al., 2020), to predict whether a pair of sentences refer to the same event or not. Later, they use these predictions as the initial scores and recalculate the pair scores by considering the relation of sentences in a pair with respect to other sentences. As the last step, final scores between these sentences are used to construct the clusters, starting with the pairs with the highest scores.

	ARI		F1	
	Macro	Micro	Macro	Micro
Örs et al.	.6006	.4644	.6736	.5898
UNC Charlotte	.3388	.3253	.4352	.3284

Table 2: Adjusted Random Index (ARI) and F1 for each baseline system.

5. Concluding Remarks

We have provided a brief summary of the workshop Automated Extraction of Socio-political Events from News (AESPEN) and the shared task Event Sentence Coreference Identification (ESCI) we organized in the scope of Language Resources and Evaluation Conference (LREC 2020). The variety of the submitted papers show that we could bring the ML, NLP, and social and political science communities together. Although the breadth of the topics were limited, the technical depth and timeliness of the contributions show that the workshop contribute to the discipline of automatic extraction of socio-political events. The papers about processing Arabic and Greek sources are significant contributions to the understanding of how should we handle languages other than English. Finally, the shared task ESCI demonstrated the prevalence of the event coreferences, some baselines for handling them, and a state-of-the-art system that is able to tackle this task.

We consider this workshop as a beginning. We expect this effort to be extended both in depth and in breadth since we think the work presented is only the tip of the iceberg considering the recent projects and technical potential introduced by deep learning technologies.

[6] https://spiderbites.nytimes.com, accessed on April 21, 2020.

6. Acknowledgements

The authors from Koç University are funded by the European Research Council (ERC) Starting Grant 714868 awarded to Dr. Erdem Yörük for his project Emerging Welfare. We appreciate contributions of the program committee members, who are in alphabetical order Svetla Boycheva, Fırat Duruşan, Theresa Gessler, Christian Göbel, Burak Gürel, Matina Halkia, Sophia Hunger, J. Craig Jenkins, Liron Lavi, Jasmine Lorenzini, Bernardo Magnini, Osman Mutlu, Nelleke Oostdijk, Arzucan Özgür, Jakub Piskorski, Lidia Pivovarova, Benjamin J. Radford, Clionadh Raleigh, Ali Safaya, Parang Saraf, Philip Schrodt, Manuela Speranza, Aline Villavicencio, Çağrı Yoltar, Kalliopi Zervanou and of the keynote speaker Clionadh Raleigh. We are grateful to the management of the Competence Centre on Text Mining and Analysis (CC-TMA) at European Commission Joint Research Center (JRC) for the support. Any opinions, findings, conclusions, or suggestions expressed here are those of the authors and do not necessarily reflect the view of the sponsor(s) or authors' employer(s).

7. Bibliographical References

Bansal, N., Blum, A., and Chawla, S. (2004). Correlation clustering. *Mach. Learn.*, 56(1–3):89–113, June.

Boschee, E., Natarajan, P., and Weischedel, R. (2013). Automatic Extraction of Events from Open Source Text for Predictive Forecasting. In V.S. Subrahmanian, editor, *Handbook of Computational Approaches to Counterterrorism*, pages 51–67. Springer New York, New York, NY.

Büyüköz, B., Hürriyetoğlu, A., and Özgür, A. (2020). Analyzing ELMo and DistilBERT on Socio-political News Classification. In *Proceedings of the Workshop Automated Extraction of Socio-political Events from News (AESPEN)*.

Chenoweth, E. and Lewis, O. A. (2013). Unpacking nonviolent campaigns: Introducing the NAVCO 2.0 dataset. *Journal of Peace Research*, 50(3):415–423.

Devlin, J., Chang, M.-W., Lee, K., and Toutanova, K. (2019). BERT: Pre-training of deep bidirectional transformers for language understanding. In *Proceedings of the 2019 Conference of the North American Chapter of the Association for Computational Linguistics: Human Language Technologies, Volume 1 (Long and Short Papers)*, pages 4171–4186, Minneapolis, Minnesota, June. Association for Computational Linguistics.

Doddington, G., Mitchell, A., Przybocki, M., Ramshaw, L., Strassel, S., and Weischedel, R. (2004). The automatic content extraction (ACE) program – tasks, data, and evaluation. In *Proceedings of the Fourth International Conference on Language Resources and Evaluation (LREC'04)*, Lisbon, Portugal, May. European Language Resources Association (ELRA).

Ettinger, A., Rao, S., Daumé III, H., and Bender, E. M. (2017). Towards Linguistically Generalizable NLP Systems: A Workshop and Shared Task. In *Proceedings of the First Workshop on Building Linguistically Generalizable NLP Systems*, pages 1–10. Association for Computational Linguistics.

Gerner, D. J., Schrodt, P. A., Yilmaz, O., and Abu-Jabr, R. (2002). Conflict and mediation event observations (cameo): A new event data framework for the analysis of foreign policy interactions. *International Studies Association, New Orleans*.

Getman, J., Ellis, J., Strassel, S., Song, Z., and Tracey, J. (2018). Laying the groundwork for knowledge base population: Nine years of linguistic resources for TAC KBP. In *Proceedings of the Eleventh International Conference on Language Resources and Evaluation (LREC 2018)*, Miyazaki, Japan, May. European Language Resources Association (ELRA).

Halkia, M., Ferri, S., Papazoglou, M., van Damme, M.-S., and Thomakos, D. (2020). Conflict Event Modelling: Research Experiment and Event Data Limitations. In *Proceedings of the Workshop Automated Extraction of Socio-political Events from News (AESPEN)*.

Hochreiter, S. and Schmidhuber, J. (1997). Long short-term memory. *Neural Computation*, 9(8):1735–1780.

Hubert, L. and Arabie, P. (1985). Comparing partitions. *Journal of classification*, 2(1):193–218.

Hürriyetoğlu, A., Yörük, E., Yüret, D., Yoltar, Ç., Gürel, B., Duruşan, F., and Mutlu, O. (2019a). A task set proposal for automatic protest information collection across multiple countries. In Leif Azzopardi, et al., editors, *Advances in Information Retrieval*, pages 316–323, Cham. Springer International Publishing.

Hürriyetoğlu, A., Yörük, E., Yüret, D., Yoltar, Ç., Gürel, B., Duruşan, F., Mutlu, O., and Akdemir, A. (2019b). Overview of clef 2019 lab protestnews: Extracting protests from news in a cross-context setting. In Fabio Crestani, et al., editors, *Experimental IR Meets Multilinguality, Multimodality, and Interaction*, pages 425–432, Cham. Springer International Publishing.

Hürriyetoğlu, A., Yörük, E., Yüret, D., Mutlu, O., Yoltar, Ç., Gürel, B., and Duruşan, F. (2020). Cross-context news corpus for protest events related knowledge base construction. In *Automated Knowledge Base Construction (AKBC)*, June.

Kriesi, H., Wüest, B., Lorenzini, J., Makarov, P., Enggist, M., Rothenhäusler, K., Kurer, T., Häusermann, Silja, P. W., Altiparmakis, A., Borbáth, E., Bremer, B., Gessler, T., Hunger, S., Hutter, S., Schulte-Cloos, J., and Wang, C. (2019). PolDem – Protest Event Dataset 30.

Lan, Z., Chen, M., Goodman, S., Gimpel, K., Sharma, P., and Soricut, R. (2020). Albert: A lite bert for self-supervised learning of language representations. In *International Conference on Learning Representations*.

Leetaru, K. and Schrodt, P. A. (2013). GDELT: Global data on events, location, and tone, 1979–2012. In *ISA annual convention*, volume 2, pages 1–49. Citeseer.

Mikolov, T., Grave, E., Bojanowski, P., Puhrsch, C., and Joulin, A. (2018). Advances in pre-training distributed word representations. In *Proceedings of the Eleventh International Conference on Language Resources and Evaluation (LREC 2018)*, Miyazaki, Japan, May. European Language Resources Association (ELRA).

Nardulli, P. F., Althaus, S. L., and Hayes, M. (2015). A Progressive Supervised-learning Approach to Generating Rich Civil Strife Data. *Sociological Methodology*, 45(1):148–183.

Olsson, F., Sahlgren, M., Abdesslem, F. B., Ekgren, A., and Eck, K. (2020). Text Categorization for Conflict Event Annotation. In *Proceedings of the Workshop Automated Extraction of Socio-political Events from News (AESPEN)*.

Örs, K. F., Yeniterzi, S., and Yeniterzi, R. (2020). Event Clustering within News Articles. In *Proceedings of the Workshop Automated Extraction of Socio-political Events from News (AESPEN)*.

Osorio, J., Reyes, A., Beltran, A., and Ahmadzai, A. (2020). Supervised Event Coding from Text Written in Arabic: Introducing Hadath. In *Proceedings of the Workshop Automated Extraction of Socio-political Events from News (AESPEN)*.

Papanikolaou, K. and Papageorgioul, H. (2020). Protest Event Analysis: A Longitudinal Analysis for Greece. In *Proceedings of the Workshop Automated Extraction of Socio-political Events from News (AESPEN)*.

Pennington, J., Socher, R., and Manning, C. (2014). Glove: Global vectors for word representation. In *Proceedings of the 2014 Conference on Empirical Methods in Natural Language Processing (EMNLP)*, pages 1532–1543, Doha, Qatar, October. Association for Computational Linguistics.

Peters, M., Neumann, M., Iyyer, M., Gardner, M., Clark, C., Lee, K., and Zettlemoyer, L. (2018). Deep contextualized word representations. In *Proceedings of the 2018 Conference of the North American Chapter of the Association for Computational Linguistics: Human Language Technologies, Volume 1 (Long Papers)*, pages 2227–2237, New Orleans, Louisiana, June. Association for Computational Linguistics.

Piskorski, J. and Jacquet, G. (2020). TF-IDF Character N-grams versusWord Embedding-based Models for Fine-grained Event Classification: A Preliminary study. In *Proceedings of the Workshop Automated Extraction of Socio-political Events from News (AESPEN)*.

Pustejovsky, J., Knippen, R., Littman, J., and Saurí, R. (2005). Temporal and event information in natural language text. *Language resources and evaluation*, 39(2-3):123–164.

Radford, B. (2020). Seeing the Forest and the Trees: Detection and Cross-Document Coreference Resolution of Militarized Interstate Disputes. In *Proceedings of the Workshop Automated Extraction of Socio-political Events from News (AESPEN).*

Raleigh, C., Linke, A., Hegre, H., and Karlsen, J. (2010). Introducing acled: an armed conflict location and event dataset: special data feature. *Journal of peace research*, 47(5):651–660.

Schrodt, P. A., Beieler, J., and Idris, M. (2014). Three'sa charm?: Open event data coding with el: Diablo, Petrarch, and the open event data alliance. In *ISA Annual Convention*.

Song, Z., Bies, A., Strassel, S., Riese, T., Mott, J., Ellis, J., Wright, J., Kulick, S., Ryant, N., and Ma, X. (2015). From light to rich ERE: Annotation of entities, relations, and events. In *Proceedings of the The 3rd Workshop on EVENTS: Definition, Detection, Coreference, and Representation*, pages 89–98, Denver, Colorado, June. Association for Computational Linguistics.

Sönmez, Ç., Özgür, A., and Yörük, E. (2016). Towards building a political protest database to explain changes in the welfare state. In *Proceedings of the 10th SIGHUM Workshop on Language Technology for Cultural Heritage, Social Sciences, and Humanities*, pages 106–110. Association for Computational Linguistics.

Wang, W., Kennedy, R., Lazer, D., and Ramakrishnan, N. (2016). Growing pains for global monitoring of societal events. *Science*, 353(6307):1502–1503.

Ward, M. D., Beger, A., Cutler, J., Dickenson, M., Dorff, C., and Radford, B. (2013). Comparing gdelt and icews event data. *Event Data Analysis*, 21(1):267–297.

Weidmann, N. B. and Rød, E. G., (2019). *The Internet and Political Protest in Autocracies*, chapter Coding Protest Events in Autocracies. Oxford Studies in Digital Politics, Oxford.

Yoruk, E. (2012). *The politics of the Turkish welfare system transformation in the neoliberal era: Welfare as mobilization and containment.* The Johns Hopkins University.

Proceedings of AESPEN 2020, page 7
Language Resources and Evaluation Conference (LREC 2020), Marseille, 11–16 May 2020

Keynote Abstract: Too soon? The limitations of AI for event data

Clionadh Raleigh
University of Sussex
5 Stoneham Road, Hove, Sussex Bn3 5hj
c.raleigh@sussex.ac.uk@abc.org

Abstract content

Not all conflict datasets offer equal levels of coverage, depth, use-ability, and content. A review of the inclusion criteria, methodology, and sourcing of leading publicly available conflict datasets demonstrates that there are significant discrepancies in the output produced by ostensibly similar projects. This keynote will question the presumption of substantial overlap between datasets, and identify a number of important gaps left by deficiencies across core criteria for effective conflict data collection and analysis, including:

Data Collection and Oversight : *A rigorous, human coder is the best way to ensure reliable, consistent, and accurate events that are not false positives.* Automated event data projects are still being refined and are not yet at the point where they can be used as accurate representations of reality. It is not appropriate to use these event datasets to present trends, maps, or distributions of violence in a state.

Inclusion : *Inclusion criteria should allow for accurate representations of political violence, while being flexible to how political violence has changed.* Who is considered a relevant and legitimate actor in conflict is pre-determined by the mandate of the dataset; the definitions, catchment, and categorization are critical, as they tell a user who and what is likely to be included.

Coverage and Classification : *Clear, coherent, and correct classifications are important for users because conflicts are not homogenous: disorder events differ in their frequency, sequences, and intensity.* Event types that reflect the variation of modalities common across conflicts and periods of disorder are basic, central components of insightful and useful analysis.

Use-ability and Transparency : *Datasets must be useful and useable if they are to be relied upon for regular analysis, and users should be able to access every detail of how conflict data are coded and collected.* Use-ability is closely tied to straightforward, consistent inclusion criteria and clear methodology.

Sourcing : *Extensive sourcing — including from local partners and media in local languages — provides the most thorough and accurate information on political violence and demonstrations, as well as the most accurate presentation of the risks that citizens and civilians experience in their homes and communities.*

Proceedings of AESPEN 2020, page 8
Language Resources and Evaluation Conference (LREC 2020), Marseille, 11–16 May 2020

Keynote Abstract: Current Open Questions for Operational Event Data

Philip A. Schrodt
Parus Analytics, LLC
Charlottesville, Virginia, USA
schrodt735@gmail.com

Abstract content

In this brief keynote, I will address what I see as five major issues in terms of development for operational event data sets (that is, event data intended for real time monitoring and forecasting, rather than purely for academic research).
First, there are no currently active real time systems with fully open and transparent pipelines: instead, one or more components are proprietary. Ideally we need several of these, using different approaches (and in particular, comparisons between classical dictionary- and rule-based coders versus newer coders based on machine-learning approaches).
Second, the CAMEO event ontology needs to be replaced by a more general system that includes, for example, political codes for electoral competition, legislative debate, and parliamentary coalition formation, as well as a robust set of codes for non-political events such as natural disasters, disease, and economic dislocations.
Third, the issue of duplicate stories needs to be addressed – for example, the ICEWS system can generate as many as 150 coded events from a single occurrence on the ground – either to reduce these sets of related stories to a single set of events, or at least to label clusters of related stories as is already done in a number of systems (for example European Media Monitor).
Fourth, a systematic analysis needs to be done as to the additional information provided by hundreds of highly local sources (which have varying degrees of varacity and independence from states and local elites) as opposed to a relatively small number of international sources: obviously this will vary depending on the specific question being asked but has yet to be addressed at all.
Finally, and this will overlap with academic work, a number of open benchmarks need to be constructed for the calibration of both coding systems and resulting models: these could be historical but need to include an easily licensed (or open) very large set of texts covering a substantial period of time, probably along the lines of the Linguistics Data Consortium Gigaword sets; if licensed, these need to be accessible to individual researchers and NGOs, not just academic institutions.

Proceedings of AESPEN 2020, pages 9–18
Language Resources and Evaluation Conference (LREC 2020), Marseille, 11–16 May 2020

Analyzing ELMo and DistilBERT on Socio-political News Classification

Berfu Büyüköz, Ali Hürriyetoğlu, Arzucan Özgür
Boğaziçi University, Koç University, Boğaziçi University
İstanbul, Turkey
{berfu.buyukoz, arzucan.ozgur}@boun.edu.tr
ahurriyetoglu@ku.edu.tr

Abstract

This study evaluates the robustness of two state-of-the-art deep contextual language representations, ELMo and DistilBERT, on supervised learning of binary protest news classification (PC) and sentiment analysis (SA) of product reviews. A "cross-context" setting is enabled using test sets that are distinct from the training data. The models are fine-tuned and fed into a Feed-Forward Neural Network (FFNN) and a Bidirectional Long Short Term Memory network (BiLSTM). Multinomial Naive Bayes (MNB) and Linear Support Vector Machine (LSVM) are used as traditional baselines. The results suggest that DistilBERT can transfer generic semantic knowledge to other domains better than ELMo. DistilBERT is also 30% smaller and 83% faster than ELMo, which suggests superiority for smaller computational training budgets. When generalization is not the utmost preference and test domain is similar to the training domain, the traditional machine learning (ML) algorithms can still be considered as more economic alternatives to deep language representations.

Keywords: deep language representations, news text classification, sentiment analysis.

1. Introduction

A challenge the Natural Language Processing (NLP) community faces today is to leverage NLP systems from a well-maintained test environment to more realistic scenarios full of dynamism and diversity (Ettinger et al., 2017; Hürriyetoğlu et al., 2019a). An NLP system should generalize well to data coming from diverse sources differing in time and space.

In the quest of building generalizable systems, the NLP community attempts building task-agnostic models in an unsupervised manner to represent generic syntactic and semantic knowledge of a language. One of the solutions is to create one big universal language representation and use it as the initialization point for any NLP task.

One example of unsupervised language representations is the famous `word2vec` (Mikolov et al., 2013), which creates continuous word vectors for each word in the vocabulary derived from a large corpus in a fully unsupervised manner by utilizing context information regarding the neighboring words. `word2vec` creates fixed vectors for each unique word in the vocabulary. In this sense, it lacks representing the dynamism of the word meaning that changes depending on the enclosing context.

The contextualization notion is the key to create universal language representations that can handle the rich syntactic and semantic space of real-life language usage. In this respect, in the last couple of years, several deep contextual neural architectures have been proposed, which have been shown to perform surprisingly well on a diverse range of downstream NLP tasks (Peters et al., 2018; Devlin et al., 2019; Radford et al., 2019).

However, there is still much to do to understand the true capacity of these representations. The true limits of these networks must be explored to understand how to build the next-generation systems. Digging into these models might even shed light on the general language understanding phenomena itself on a cognitive level (Greenwood, 1992; Kell et al., 2018). For this reason, exhaustive evaluation and interpretation studies are needed to be performed on as many different data and task sets as possible.

This study is conducted to contribute to the extrinsic evaluation of the robustness of two of these representations, namely, ELMo and DistilBERT, by testing them on a binary classification of cross-context socio-political and local news data, where the source and target data differ in the originating country and domain (Hürriyetoğlu et al., 2019a).

This study aims to answer the following questions:

1. How robust are ELMo and DistilBERT in the cross-context socio-political news classification?
2. Are contextual representations better in the cross-context than much smaller and faster traditional baselines?
3. Which one is more scalable in terms of model size and training time: ELMo or DistilBERT?

The following conclusions are reached under the limitations of the experimental setup (See Section 3.):

1. DistilBERT is more robust than ELMo in the cross-context.
2. Both ELMo and DistilBERT outperform the baselines, namely, Multinomial Naive Bayes (MNB) and Linear Support Vector Machine (LSVM), in generalizing to the cross-context.
3. DistilBERT is more efficient than ELMo with 30% smaller size and on average for the two addressed tasks, 83% faster training and testing time.
4. Traditional methods like MNB and LSVM can still compete with contextual embeddings when training and test data do not differ much.

This study compares language representations and model performance on both a sentiment analysis task and a recently proposed task set that is realized around a recent news data set: classifying protest news on local news data sets consisting of multiple sentences and coming from different country sources. A "cross-country" evaluation setting is realized by testing a model on a news text coming from a different country than the training data (Hürriyetoğlu et al., 2019a). While this study is one among many that compare word representations for text classification, this study diverges from most previous works by evaluating cross-context performance in a novel domain.

2. Tasks and Data

The transfer capacity of ELMo and DistilBERT are explored under the light of two distinct text classification tasks, each realized under a cross-context experimental setting. One is a document-level binary text classification task that is to classify English news articles from local newspapers of India and China (Hürriyetoğlu et al., 2019a). The other is to classify sentence-level Rotten Tomatoes movie (Pang and Lee, 2005) and customer reviews (Hu and Liu, 2004).

The "null context" refers to the India news and movie reviews data sets. The "cross-context" refers to the China news and customer reviews data sets. For both tasks, the null context data splits abide by the 75% - 10% - 15% proportions for training, test, and development sets, respectively. All cross-context data are used to test models trained on null-context data's train portion.

2.1. Protest News Classification

The task was designed as an auxiliary task for an active research project (Hürriyetoğlu et al., 2019a), the main motivation of which is to automate creation of protest events database from diverse sources using NLP and Machine Learning (ML) to enable a comparative political and sociological study. A shared task set, namely, CLEF-2019 Lab ProtestNews on Extracting Protests from News, was accordingly organized to address the challenge of building NLP tools that are generalizable to different test data. A cross-country evaluation setting was realized by training a model on local newspapers of India and testing the model on local newspapers of China.

The data consists of local India and China document-level news articles in the English language. Training, validation, and test splits are provided by the shared task organizers. Each news article is annotated as whether it is about a protest event or not. As illustrated in Table 1, the India data is imbalanced with 22% protest class, the China data is even more imbalanced with 5% protest class.

Data Subset	Size	Protest Ratio
Ntrain	3430	0.22
Ndev	457	0.22
Ntest	687	0.22
Ctest	1800	0.05

Table 1: Protest news data statistics. Ntrain, Ndev, and Ntest refer to training, development, and test splits of the null context data of the tasks, respectively. Ctest refers to the cross-context data.

2.2. Challenges of Political Context

In previous work, it is seen that the classification of contentious political events could be confusing to even domain experts and the inter-annotator agreement could be surprisingly low (King and Lowe, 2003). That confusion mostly comes from the ambiguity in political terms. How a political event could be interpreted can highly depend on local culture, language usage, time, space and actors. Adding the style and biases of the author of the news text, even a single annotator may not be completely sure of his/her annotations, let alone agreeing with fellow annotators.

Within the context of contentious politics, "protest" can be very broadly defined as engaging in a political dissent via numerous actions such as demonstrating for rights, rallying for political change, conducting a hunger strike, boycotting rights, and so forth.

Members of the Communist Party of India (Marxist) staged a **protest** here on Thursday **demanding** the arrest of the remaining accused in the last month's assault on party-goers at the Morning Mist Homestay in Padil and filing of cases under the **Goonda Act** against them. The protest meeting was preceded by a rally from Town Hall to ...

Figure 1: India news sample.

2.2.1. Local News Data

Political events are strongly connected to their local context. Concerning protest news classification (PC), it should be noted that protests might manifest through different kinds of actions in different cultures. In Figure 1, the news mentions a protest activity as "Goonda act", which is a term used in the Indian subcontinent for a hired criminal. In this sense, analyzing local data of many countries can be useful and mostly becomes a necessity to converge to a realistic model of what protest means both globally and locally.

2.2.2. Small Data

Contextual language representations are known to have the potential to substantially reduce the required training data size to create satisfactory models via task-specific finetuning on small data. As illustrated in Table 1. the protest news data is also fairly small, with the number of training samples less than 10000 (both local and cross-country data sets).

2.2.3. Long Text

The protest news data set consists of fairly long samples with 300 tokens on average.[1] This may affect the model performance in two different ways: A model may fail to learn long term relationships within the text or a model may simply not be able to utilize the whole text due to memory

[1]Here,"token" is used as a generic term for a unit output of a sequence tokenization process.

issues. In this case, very important parts of the data might be lost. For example, the news sample in Figure 2 was classified falsely as "non-protest", since the "protest" keyword was clipped due to the limitation to maximum number of tokens.

> Police classed as criminal an explosion that killed a **car** driver in Wuhan yesterday - the second lethal vehicle **explosion** in the central city in nearly three months, state media said. Xinhua reported a black car belonging to a Bank of China branch in the city exploded and burst into flames shortly before mid-day as it was being driven near the junction of Qianjin 4th Road and Zizhi Street
>
> ...It was not clear if the explosion was related to the bank or a **protest** of the recent ban on direct sales by the Government. It was reported that many sales agents in Wuhan had **protested** against the ban. Another unconfirmed report said the explosion might have been the act of laid-off workers.

Figure 2: China news sample.

2.3. Sentiment Analysis

The other task addressed in this paper is to classify sentence-level Rotten Tomatoes movie (MR) (Pang and Lee, 2005) and customer reviews (CR) (Hu and Liu, 2004) as "positive" or "negative". The models are trained and tested on sentence-level MR (Pang and Lee, 2005) in the null context, and tested on sentence-level CR (Hu and Liu, 2004) in the cross-context.

Both sentiment data sets were exhaustively used earlier (Kiros et al., 2015; Zhao et al., 2015; Conneau et al., 2017; Conneau and Kiela, 2018; Logeswaran and Lee, 2018; Hill et al., 2016). But in none of these studies a cross-context setting is realized. They obtained the result via direct supervision on the target tasks.

Data Subset	Size	Positive Ratio
Ntrain	7974	0.5
Ndev	1088	0.5
Ntest	1600	0.5
Ctest	3771	0.64

Table 2: Sentiment data statistics. Ntrain: Training split of MR data set. Ndev: Development split of MR data set. Ntest: Test split of MR data set. Ctest: CR data set as the cross-context test data.

3. Experimental Setup

Four experiments are applied to better understand the cross-context performance of the models. The classifiers are implemented in the Python programming language using the PyTorch library.[2]

[2] `https://pytorch.org/`

3.1. ELMo

ELMo (Peters et al., 2018) is a deep context-dependent representation learned from the internal states of a deep bidirectional language model that is acquired by the joint training of two LSTM layers on both directions. This study makes use of the original pretrained ELMo model with 2 layer bidirectional LSTM layers with 4096 units and 512-dimensional projections, with a total of 93.6 million parameters. ELMo's hidden LSTM layers are weighted averaged and then fed into the classifier layers.

3.2. DistilBERT

DistilBERT (Sanh et al., 2019) is created by applying knowledge distillation to BERT (Devlin et al., 2019), specifically the `bert-base-uncased` model. To create a smaller version of BERT, DistilBERT's creators removed the token-type embeddings and the pooler from the architecture and reduced the number of layers by a factor of 2. In this study, DistilBERT's last four hidden layers are simply averaged and fed into the classifier layers, which is a suggested usage of BERT for text classification tasks.

In this study, `distilbert-base-uncased`[3] with 66 million parameters is compared to the original ELMo model with 93.6 million parameters.[4]

3.3. Classifiers

The classifier architectures are kept simple to focus on what information can be easily extracted from ELMo and DistilBERT. First, a 2-layer FFNN with 512 hidden units is used. Then, to better understand the effect of adding task-trained contextualization, a 2-layer BiLSTM with 512 hidden units is added before the linear output layer. The default maximum sequence length is 256 tokens for PC, 60 tokens for SA. ELMo gets that many full tokens, whereas DistilBERT gets that many WordPiece (Wu et al., 2016) outputs. The architectures are visualized in Figure 3.

3.4. Baseline Models

Optimized LSVM and MNB scores are reported as baselines.[5] LSVM takes the input as tf-idf (term frequency - inverse document frequency) vectors, whereas MNB as a sparse vector of token counts.

The baseline models are much simpler than the neural classifiers described in Figure 3. The baseline models utilize simple word representations which do not preserve word order and context information. By comparing traditional ML algorithms to heavily pretrained large contextual networks, we aim at understanding if the overhead of the deep contextual models is worth to undertake in this task.

3.5. Tokenization

Except for DistilBERT, the sequences are tokenized by Spacy's `en-core-web-sm` tokenizer[6]. DistilBERT uses

[3] `https://github.com/huggingface/transformers`

[4] `https://allennlp.org/elmo`, accessed in March 2020.

[5] `https://scikit-learn.org/stable/`, accessed in March 2020.

[6] `https://spacy.io/`.

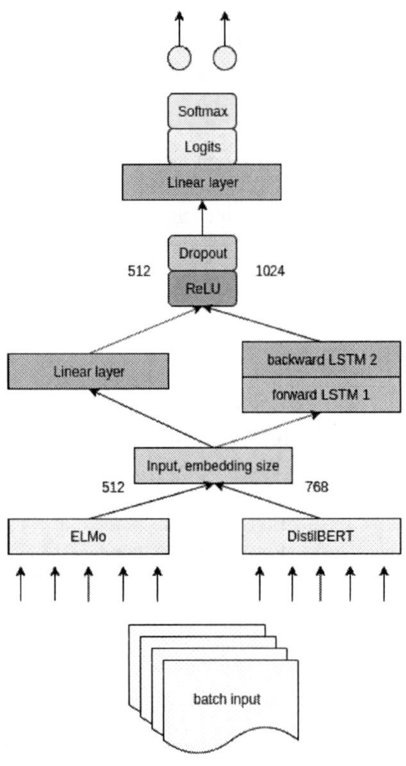

Figure 3: Classifier architecture. These are two distinct classifiers only visualized intersecting on the common layers.

WordPiece tokenization. The first 256 tokens and 60 tokens per sample are given as input to the classifiers for the PC and sentiment analysis (SA) tasks, respectively. Note that the usage of two different tokenizers causes a mismatch between the input of DistilBERT and other models. But WordPiece tokenization is preferred for DistilBERT as it is the default tokenizer of it. No text pre-processing is performed on the texts (such as casing, stop word removal, stemming, etc.). Out-of-sample tokens are not specially treated in training FFNN and BiLSTM since ELMo and DistilBERT already take care of those: the former with character-based tokenization, the latter with WordPiece tokenization. In baseline models, out-of-vocabulary tokens were simply not propagated to the classifier.

3.6. Hyper-parameter Tuning

The hyper-parameters of each distinct model are optimized on the validation data with the Tree-structured Parzen Estimator algorithm. The implementation of the algorithm is provided by the hyperopt package.[7]

The hyper-parameter tuning for the baselines was straightforward, for there were few possible hyper-parameters to be tuned as seen in Table 4.

[7] `https://github.com/hyperopt/hyperopt`, accessed in March 2020.

HParam	Range
learning rate	5e-5, 1e-3, 1e-1
learning rate decay	0, 0.5
dropout	0, 0.25, 0.5
L2	0, 0.01
Use ReLu?	True, False

Table 3: Hyper-parameter space.

Model	HParam	Range
MNB	alpha	0, 0.25, 0.5, 0.75, 1
MNB	fit-prior	True, False
LSVM	loss	hinge, squared hinge
LSVM	tolerance	1e-2, 1e-3, 1e-4
LSVM	C	0.5, 1

Table 4: Hyper-parameter space of the baselines.

3.7. Training

The training is done on a single V100 NVIDIA GPU with 16 GB RAM. The classifiers are trained for 10 epochs with the Adam optimizer (Kingma and Ba, 2014) using step decay with the patience of 3 epochs. The best model is checkpointed regarding the development set F-score. Then the checkpoints are evaluated on the test data. This procedure is repeated for each classifier with 5 random seeds and the average scores are reported.

3.8. Experiments

All experiments report both null and cross-context results for each task. Each experiment focuses on a particular variation on the classifier architecture that possibly affects the results in its way. First, both ELMo and DistilBERT are used as fixed (with *frozen* weights) word vectors and fed into FFNN. Then, they are fine-tuned to the training data sets together with the FFNN classifier. In the third setting, both models are kept *frozen* (the weights of the language models are not updated during training), but this time paired with a BiLSTM instead of an FFNN. Lastly, they are compared under the combined effect of fine-tuning contextual embeddings and pairing with a 2-layer BiLSTM.

Macro averaged F-score ($\beta = 1$) is used as the primary evaluation metric in both tasks since it provides a more robust evaluation for class-imbalanced data. Also as an additional metric, the F-score drop between null and cross-context is tracked in percentages. That is, for example, if model x null context F-score is f_n and its cross-context setting F-score is f_c, then the drop in F-score is calculated as $(f_n - c_n)/f_n * 100$. This metric helps reveal the true cross-context performance in some cases where absolute F-scores fail to do so.

The dropout rate of the classifier (FFNN or BiLSTM), learning rate, learning rate decay, L2 norm, and whether to use ReLU or not, are the hyper-parameters that were tuned for each model. Hyper-parameters of ELMo and DistilBERT are kept unchanged.

4. Experiment Results

In this section, ELMo and DistilBERT are compared using various classification architectures on two cross-context

text classification tasks.

4.1. Experiment 1 - Frozen Embeddings

Table 5 shows that frozen DistilBERT is on par with or exceeding frozen ELMo in the null context (India and MR test sets). On the other hand, DistilBERT outperforms ELMo in the cross-contexts (China and CR sets) with a smaller "Drop" score in both tasks.

Task	Model	Ntest	Ctest	Drop
PC	ELMo 256	83.6	75.2	10
PC	DBERT 256	**83.8**	**76.8**	**8.2**
SA	ELMo	78	63.6	18.4
SA	DBERT	**79**	**66.8**	**15.4**

Table 5: Experiment 1 results. Frozen ELMo and DistilBERT combined with FFNN.

4.2. Experiment 2 - Fine-tuned Embeddings

In this stage, ELMo and DistilBERT are fine-tuned on the training data sets together with the FFNN classifier.
Fine-tuned ELMo does not fit into a single GPU with 256 tokens per input sample. In this case, ELMo could manage up to 150 tokens per input. For a fair comparison, DistilBERT is trained twice, first with 150 tokens of input, and then as a separate model, with 256 tokens of input.

Task	Model	Ntest	Ctest	Drop
PC	ELMo ft 150	83	72.2	13
PC	DBERT ft 150	80	71	11.3
PC	DBERT ft 256	**83.2**	**76.4**	**8.2**
SA	ELMo ft	76.2	**69**	**9.6**
SA	DBERT ft	**79**	68	14

Table 6: Experiment 2 results. Fine-tuned ELMo and DistilBERT combined with FFNN.

As illustrated in Table 6, when the context is restricted to 150 tokens, fine-tuned ELMo outperforms DistilBERT, but falls behind in 256 tokens especially in cross-context. On the other hand, in SA, DistilBERT surpasses ELMo in the null context, but falls behind in the cross-context. This indicates that in SA, fine-tuning made ELMo more robust to context change in the test set.

4.3. Experiment 3 - External Contextualization via BiLSTM

In this experiment, both models are kept frozen, but this time paired with a BiLSTM instead of an FFNN. BiLSTM adds contextualization on the focused task, thus it is expected to improve results.

Task	Model	Ntest	Ctest	Drop
PC	ELMo 256	81.6	72.4	11.2
PC	DBERT 256	**84.2**	**78.4**	**7**
SA	ELMo	79	67	15.2
SA	DBERT	**80**	**70.2**	**12.4**

Table 7: Experiment 3 results. Frozen ELMo and DistilBERT combined with BiLSTM.

As Table 7 illustrates, in both tasks DistilBERT outperforms ELMo when paired with a 2-layer BiLSTM. The gap is more visible in the cross-context performance: DistilBERT surpasses ELMo 6 points with a 78.4 Ctest F-score on the PC task.

4.4. Experiment 4 - Combining Fine-tuning with BiLSTM

In this experiment, ELMo and DistilBERT are compared under the combined effect of fine-tuning and the usage of 2-layer BiLSTM. In PC, ELMo could handle at most 150 tokens per input. Therefore, the comparison is done under that much of a sequence length.

Task	Model	Ntest	Ctest	Drop
PC	ELMo ft 150	**82**	72	12.2
PC	DBERT ft 150	81.8	**72.2**	**11.8**
SA	ELMo ft	78.2	67.4	13.8
SA	DBERT ft	**80**	**70.2**	**12.4**

Table 8: Experiment 4 results. Fine-tuned ELMo and DistilBERT combined with BiLSTM.

In Experiment 2, DistilBERT was underperforming on sequences of length 150 in PC. Now, as illustrated in Table 8 DistilBERT catches up with ELMo. This indicates that DistilBERT benefits from BiLSTM.

4.5. Comparison to Baselines

For fairness, both ELMo's and DistilBERT's best and worst-performing configurations are compared to the hyper-parameter-tuned MNB and LSVM baselines. The best performing models are indicated with the keywords "highest", the worst-performing with "lowest" in Table 10. Two models are reported as the "highest" of ELMo in SA as one owns better "Drop" scores.

Task	Model Tag	Model Name
PC	ELMo (lowest)	ELMo + BiLSTM 256
PC	ELMo (highest)	ELMo 256
PC	DBERT (lowest)	DBERT ft 256 (lowest)
PC	DBERT (highest)	DBERT 256
SA	ELMo (lowest)	ELMo
SA	ELMo (highest 1)	ELMo ft
SA	ELMo (highest 2)	ELMo + BiLSTM
SA	DBERT (lowest)	DBERT
SA	DBERT (highest)	DBERT ft + BiLSTM

Table 9: Names of worst and best performing models.

Table 10 demonstrates that in PC, while LSVM cannot catch up with any model, MNB performs fairly on par with ELMo's worst-performing model. Apart from that, MNB is effectively surpassed by the best of ELMo and DistilBERT in all categories. In SA, MNB is inferior to all models. The results of LSVM and ELMo's lowest are close to each other. But the best of ELMo and all variants of DistilBERT surpass the LSVM baseline with an apparent gap in the cross-context robustness.
It is also visible that DistilBERT outperforms ELMo on both tasks with both of its worst-performing and best-

Task	Model	Ntest	Ctest	Drop
PC	LSVM 256	79	64	19
PC	MNB 256	80	73	9
PC	ELMo (lowest)	81.6	72.4	11.2
PC	ELMo (highest)	83.6	75.2	10
PC	DBERT (lowest)	83.2	76.4	**8.2**
PC	DBERT (highest)	**83.8**	**76.8**	**8.2**
SA	MNB	78	57	27
SA	LSVM	77	62	19
SA	ELMo (lowest)	78	63.6	18.4
SA	ELMo (highest 1)	76.2	69	**9.6**
SA	ELMo (highest 2)	79	67	15.2
SA	DBERT (lowest)	79	66.8	15.4
SA	DBERT (highest)	**80**	**70.2**	12.4

Table 10: Comparison with the baselines.

performing variants. This can be viewed as an indicator of the possible superiority of DistilBERT.

4.6. Average Scores

To view the experiments from a wider perspective, the models are also compared under the arithmetic average of all variations. As Table 11 displays, ELMo is found to be superior to DistilBERT on average when both use only 150 tokens of protest news input.[8] But in SA when full context is available DistilBERT performs better regardless of short sequence length. On average of common variations, DistilBERT is dominant in both tasks. This can be seen as an indicator of DistilBERT's overall superiority.

Task	Average	Ntest	Ctest	Drop
PC	ELMo 150	81.95	73.25	10.55
PC	DBERT 150	80.95	72.8	10
PC	ELMo	**82.17**	73.43	10.57
PC	DBERT	81.97	**74.4**	**9.2**
SA	ELMo	77.85	66.75	14.25
SA	DBERT	**79.5**	**68.8**	**13.6**

Table 11: Average scores of ELMo and DistilBERT.

4.7. Training Time and Model Size

Training times and model sizes are compared by averaging all model configurations common to ELMo and DistilBERT. Training and inference time are summed up to a single number. According to Table 12, DistilBERT is 30% smaller and 83% faster than ELMo on the average of both tasks. In terms of classifier size (excluding embeddings) DistilBERT is 13% smaller than ELMo. On the other hand, MNB and LSVM are far more efficient than DistilBERT in size and speed by being 99% smaller and 96% faster.

4.8. New State-of-the-art in CLEF-2019 Lab ProtestNews

Combining contextual embeddings with standard shallow neural networks (FFNN and BiLSTM) and applying hyper-

[8]For fairness, DistilBERT's fine-tuned models making use of 256 length input are excluded from the computation because there is no equivalent model on the ELMo side.

Task	Model	ESize	MSize	Ttime
PC	MNB	-	**1.1**	**12**
PC	ELMo	358	75.55	1690
PC	DBERT	254	65.8	318
SA	LSVM	-	**0.133**	**10**
SA	ELMo	358	75.55	979
SA	DBERT	254	65.8	237

Table 12: Average training time and model sizes of ELMo and DistilBERT. ESize: Embedding size. MSize: Model size. TTime: Train time. Sizes are in Megabytes. Train time is in seconds.

parameter tuning helped outrun the prior results in the CLEF-2019 Lab ProtestNews in cross-context while getting comparable results in null context. As shown in Table 13, F-score in China test set increased from 65 to 76.8 F-score; "Drop" is diminished from 22% to 8.2%.

Model	Ntest	Ctest	Drop
(Radford, 2019)	83	65	22
DBERT 256	**83.8**	**76.8**	**8.2**

Table 13: Comparison with CLEF-2019 Lab ProtestNews results. The prior state-of-the-art is exceeded in cross-context.

5. Randomization Test

The randomization test (Yeh, 2000) is applied to the results to check if the models significantly differ in terms of scores. The randomization test is performed by calculating p-values for all combinations of predictions obtained by training with different seeds. For example, when two models of ELMo and DistilBERT are compared, 25 different p-values are produced by using 25 different pairs of 5 ELMo and 5 DistilBERT outcomes. The harmonic mean of these p-values is used as the ultimate statistic of the test to smooth the disproportional effect of large p-values occuring in arithmetic mean.

The harmonic mean of a series equals to zero if the series contains any zero value. For more realistic evaluation, the harmonic mean of non-zero p-values are also reported (Ntest-p, Ctest-p, Drop-p). For example, if a randomization output contains at least one zero value, the true harmonic mean becomes automatically zero. In that case, we also include the harmonic mean found after excluding zero values. The results are reported in Tables 14 and 15 by separating those alternative results by / (e.g. 0/0.01). Nevertheless, zero values should not be entirely ignored since their existence points out that rejection of the null hypothesis is indeed very much probable.

It should be noted that for PC two-tailed randomization tests general statistics (both positive and negative class) show that there is no significant difference between ELMo and DistilBERT's Ntest and Ctest performance ($p = 0.38$ and $p = 0.59$, respectively). But, since negative class ratio is much larger than positive class ratio in protest news data (see Table 1), it dominates two-tailed tests. We conducted one-tailed test only with positive (protest) class instances in PC task to get more realistic results for the positive class. Tables 14 and 15 suggest that, according to the randomization tests, DistilBERT is significantly better ($\alpha = 0.05$) in both null and cross-context for positive class in PC and both classes in SA. ELMo, in turn, is observed to be superior to the baselines in cross-context. But ELMo is on par with the baselines in null context.

Models	Task	Ntest-p	Ctest-p	Drop-p
ELMo-DBERT	PC	**0/0.01**	**0/0.004**	**0/0.006**
ELMo-MNB	PC	**0.007**	**0/0.009**	**0.004**

Table 14: PC - One-tailed randomization test p-value results on the best performing model variations of ELMo, DistilBERT, and MNB. A value is made bold if it can reject the null hypothesis. Ntest-p, Ctest-p, and Drop-p stand for "positive (protest) class statistics."

Models	Task	Ctest	Drop
ELMo-DBERT	SA	**0/0.017**	**0.02/0.02**
ELMo-LSVM	SA	**0/0**	**0/0.009**

Table 15: SA - One-tailed randomization test p-value results on the best performing model variations of ELMo, DistilBERT, and LSVM. A value is made bold if it can reject the null hypothesis.

6. Related Work

This section overviews the previous work that is focused on understanding the generalization capacity of the contextual language representations.

6.1. Evaluating Transfer Capacity of Language Models

The evaluation studies before this work are generally designed around a diverse set of downstream tasks (Devlin et al., 2019; Liu et al., 2019; Tenney et al., 2019; Peters et al., 2019) or ablation studies (Liu et al., 2019). Sun et al. (2019) focus on the effective tuning methods of pretrained representations, while Howard and Ruder (2018) propose a set of parameter tuning techniques specifically to leverage text classification performance. Han and Eisenstein (2019) apply unsupervised domain adaptation by further pretraining contextual representations on the masked language model on the target domain. Tenney et al. (2019) observed that contextual embeddings substantially improve over traditional baselines on learning the syntactic structure of text, but that there is only a small improvement in learning semantics on token and sentence level tasks.

6.2. Cross-context Protest Event Text Analysis

A task set (Hürriyetoğlu et al., 2019a) was proposed to collect protest event information from news texts to create systems that learn transferable information to extract relevant information from multiple countries with the ultimate motivation to create tools to enable comparative sociology and political studies on social protest phenomena. The task set consists of three tasks: news articles classification, event sentence detection, and event information extraction.

The protest news classification task was realized in the CLEF-2019 Lab ProtestNews on Extracting Protests from News (Hürriyetoğlu et al., 2019c) in the context of generalizable natural language processing[9]. From the results gathered from 12 teams, it was observed that Neural Networks obtained the best results and a significant drop in cross-country performance is observed on the news from China (Hürriyetoğlu et al., 2019b). The best performing model on average for the null and cross-context trained a BiLSTM with `fastText` (Joulin et al., 2017; Mikolov et al., 2018) embeddings on a multitask learning objective (Radford, 2019). Safaya (2019) attained the smallest score drop between null and cross-contexts using BiGRU and `word2vec`. Another study utilized ELMo with a fully connected multi-layer Neural Network, reaching comparable results (Maslennikova, 2019).

6.3. Sentiment Analysis

Sentiment analysis is a frequently studied classification task. MR and CR are a couple of exhaustively used data sets for this task. Successful models on this task involve combining `word2vec` with self-adaptive hierarchical sentence representations (Zhao et al., 2015); sentence representations that are learned by supervised training on a Natural Language Inference data (Conneau et al., 2017; Bowman et al., 2015); and a multi-channel system consisting of two bi-directional recurrent neural networks fed by tunable word vectors (Logeswaran and Lee, 2018).

7. Discussion

DistilBERT is better at utilizing longer sequences than ELMo. Fine-tuned ELMo cannot handle as many tokens as DistilBERT can, due to excessive RAM usage. This deteriorates ELMo's performance, especially in the cross-context. Moreover, fine-tuning causes training ELMo to take 1.5X longer, while the effect is negligible in DistilBERT.

Null context performance and cross-context performance do not necessarily grow together. For some specific configurations, when DistilBERT outran ELMo in the null context, ELMo happened to outperform DistilBERT in the cross-context or vice versa. Similarly, fine-tuning could improve null context performance, but caused a drop in the cross-context performance. Even usage of longer context can cause such an effect. These observations indicate that it is important to check the robustness of a model on multiple dimensions to understand true generalization power.

It should be emphasized that the limitations of the experimental setup and the scope must always be noted when the observations of this study are concerned. All conclusions are valid only under the specific experimental setup of this study, comprising the aforementioned binary classification tasks and the data sets. The results might be completely different, even in the case when the models are pretrained with

[9]`http://clef2019.clef-initiative.eu/`, accessed in December 2019.

other corpora. So it must be underlined that the comparison results are special to the model-unlabeled data combinations (ELMo combined with One Billion Word Benchmark, DistilBERT combined with English Wikipedia and Toronto BookCorpus).

8. Conclusion

In this study, ELMo and DistilBERT are compared on their fine-tuning performance on two binary text classification tasks. The main focus was to see how much can these models be benefited from in a practical way without any modification to the pretraining outputs.

Overall, DistilBERT is found to generalize better than ELMo on the cross-context setting. While DistilBERT and ELMo seem to have close performance in terms of absolute F-score, DistilBERT apparently outperforms ELMo in F-score drop in percentages. In addition, DistilBERT is 30% smaller in embedding size and 83% faster in training time than ELMo. No significant difference could be detected between ELMo and DistilBERT in the null context. The baselines are outran by both models in the cross-context robustness. But the baselines could occasionally get comparable results with ELMo in the null context. Also, they are very economic with 99% smaller size and 96% faster training and testing time when compared to DistilBERT.

As a result, when the transfer power of a model is a priority, it is worth to prefer contextual neural models over traditional ML methods despite much longer training times and memory overhead. On the other hand, traditional ML methods might still be preferred as low-cost options when there is no anticipated discrepancy between training and test data.

9. Future Work

The main focus in this study was to compare ELMo and DistilBERT without any intervention to the pretrained models, although the models were actually pretrained on entirely different corpora - ELMo on One Billion Words Benchmark (Chelba et al., 2013), DistilBERT on English Wikipedia and Toronto BookCorpus (Zhu et al., 2015). If the models were also pretrained from scratch on the same corpus, it would be ensured that they utilize the same knowledge to learn the context. This would enable a fairer comparison.

By leveraging unsupervised data into training, classifiers could adapt to many different cross-context settings more effectively and much faster. Unsupervised domain adaptation seems to be a wise direction to take (Han and Eisenstein, 2019).

Currently NLP evaluation and comparison studies are realized under varying conditions defined by specific priorities and research interests of every other study, including this particular one. This prevents making proper comparisons between observations of studies, which could enable progress based on a much more confident common ground. Defining standard evaluation pipelines to be adopted within the NLP field in general can be a way to overcome this dilemma.

10. Acknowledgements

We are grateful to Koç University Emerging Markets Welfare research team, which is funded by the European Research Council (ERC) Starting Grant 714868 awarded to Dr. Erdem Yörük for their generosity in providing the data and sharing invaluable insight. We thank the Text Analytics and Bioinformatics (TABI) Lab members in Boğaziçi University for their inspiring feedback and support. The numerical calculations reported in this paper were partially performed at TUBITAK ULAKBIM, High Performance and Grid Computing Center (TRUBA resources). GEBIP Award of the Turkish Academy of Sciences (to A.O.) is gratefully acknowledged

11. Bibliographical References

Bowman, S. R., Angeli, G., Potts, C., and Manning, C. D. (2015). A large annotated corpus for learning natural language inference. In *Proceedings of the 2015 Conference on Empirical Methods in Natural Language Processing*, pages 632–642, Lisbon, Portugal, September. Association for Computational Linguistics.

Chelba, C., Mikolov, T., Schuster, M., Ge, Q., Brants, T., Koehn, P., and Robinson, T. (2013). One billion word benchmark for measuring progress in statistical language modeling. Technical report, Google.

Conneau, A. and Kiela, D. (2018). SentEval: An evaluation toolkit for universal sentence representations. In *Proceedings of the Eleventh International Conference on Language Resources and Evaluation (LREC 2018)*, Miyazaki, Japan, May. European Language Resources Association (ELRA).

Conneau, A., Kiela, D., Schwenk, H., Barrault, L., and Bordes, A. (2017). Supervised learning of universal sentence representations from natural language inference data. In *Proceedings of the 2017 Conference on Empirical Methods in Natural Language Processing*, pages 670–680, Copenhagen, Denmark, September. Association for Computational Linguistics.

Devlin, J., Chang, M.-W., Lee, K., and Toutanova, K. (2019). BERT: Pre-training of deep bidirectional transformers for language understanding. In *Proceedings of the 2019 Conference of the North American Chapter of the Association for Computational Linguistics: Human Language Technologies, Volume 1 (Long and Short Papers)*, pages 4171–4186, Minneapolis, Minnesota, June. Association for Computational Linguistics.

Ettinger, A., Rao, S., Daumé III, H., and Bender, E. M. (2017). Towards linguistically generalizable NLP systems: A workshop and shared task. In *Proceedings of the First Workshop on Building Linguistically Generalizable NLP Systems*, pages 1–10, Copenhagen, Denmark, September. Association for Computational Linguistics.

Greenwood, A. (1992). Computational neuroscience: A window to understanding how the brain works. In *Science at the Frontier*, chapter 9, pages 199–232. The National Academies Press, Washington, DC.

Han, X. and Eisenstein, J. (2019). Unsupervised domain adaptation of contextualized embeddings for sequence labeling. *arXiv:1907.11692.*

Hill, F., Cho, K., and Korhonen, A. (2016). Learning distributed representations of sentences from unlabelled data. In *Proceedings of the 2016 Conference of the North American Chapter of the Association for Computational Linguistics: Human Language Technologies*, pages 1367–1377, San Diego, California, June. Association for Computational Linguistics.

Howard, J. and Ruder, S. (2018). Universal language model fine-tuning for text classification. In *Proceedings of the 56th Annual Meeting of the Association for Computational Linguistics (Volume 1: Long Papers)*, pages 328–339, Melbourne, Australia, July. Association for Computational Linguistics.

Hu, M. and Liu, B. (2004). Mining and summarizing customer reviews. In *Proceedings of the Tenth ACM SIGKDD International Conference on Knowledge Discovery and Data Mining*, KDD '04, pages 168–177, New York, NY, USA. ACM.

Hürriyetoğlu, A., Yörük, E., Yüret, D., Yoltar, Ç., Gürel, B., Duruşan, F., and Mutlu, O. (2019a). A task set proposal for automatic protest information collection across multiple countries. In Leif Azzopardi, et al., editors, *Advances in Information Retrieval*, pages 316–323, Cham. Springer International Publishing.

Hürriyetoğlu, A., Yörük, E., Yüret, D., Yoltar, Ç., Gürel, B., Duruşan, F., Mutlu, O., and Akdemir, A. (2019b). Overview of clef 2019 lab protestnews: Extracting protests from news in a cross-context setting. In Fabio Crestani, et al., editors, *Experimental IR Meets Multilinguality, Multimodality, and Interaction*, pages 425–432, Cham. Springer International Publishing.

Hürriyetoğlu, A., Yörük, E., Yüret, D., Yörük, E., Yoltar, Ç., Gürel, B., Duruşan, F., Mutlu, O., Akdemir, A., Gessler, T., and Makarov, P., (2019c). *CLEF-2019 Lab ProtestNews on Extracting Protests from News*. accessed in December 2019.

Joulin, A., Grave, E., Bojanowski, P., and Mikolov, T. (2017). Bag of tricks for efficient text classification. In *Proceedings of the 15th Conference of the European Chapter of the Association for Computational Linguistics: Volume 2, Short Papers*, pages 427–431, Valencia, Spain, April. Association for Computational Linguistics.

Kell, A. J., Yamins, D. L., Shook, E. N., Norman-Haignere, S. V., and McDermott, J. H. (2018). A task-optimized neural network replicates human auditory behavior, predicts brain responses, and reveals a cortical processing hierarchy. *Neuron*, 98(3):630 – 644.e16.

King, G. and Lowe, W. (2003). An automated information extraction tool for international conflict data with performance as good as human coders: A rare events evaluation design. *International Organization*, 57:617–642, July.

Kingma, D. and Ba, J. (2014). Adam: A method for stochastic optimization. *International Conference on Learning Representations*, 12.

Kiros, R., Zhu, Y., Salakhutdinov, R. R., Zemel, R., Urtasun, R., Torralba, A., and Fidler, S. (2015). Skip-thought vectors. In C. Cortes, et al., editors, *Advances in Neural Information Processing Systems 28*, pages 3294–3302. Curran Associates, Inc.

Liu, N. F., Gardner, M., Belinkov, Y., Peters, M. E., and Smith, N. A. (2019). Linguistic knowledge and transferability of contextual representations. In *Proceedings of the 2019 Conference of the North American Chapter of the Association for Computational Linguistics: Human Language Technologies, Volume 1 (Long and Short Papers)*, pages 1073–1094, Minneapolis, Minnesota, June. Association for Computational Linguistics.

Logeswaran, L. and Lee, H. (2018). An efficient framework for learning sentence representations. In *International Conference on Learning Representations*.

Maslennikova, E. (2019). Elmo word representations for news protection. *In Working Notes of CLEF 2019 - Conference and Labs of the Evaluation Forum*, 07.

Mikolov, T., Sutskever, I., Chen, K., Corrado, G. S., and Dean, J. (2013). Distributed representations of words and phrases and their compositionality. In C. J. C. Burges, et al., editors, *Advances in Neural Information Processing Systems 26*, pages 3111–3119. Curran Associates, Inc.

Mikolov, T., Grave, E., Bojanowski, P., Puhrsch, C., and Joulin, A. (2018). Advances in pre-training distributed word representations. In *Proceedings of the International Conference on Language Resources and Evaluation (LREC 2018)*.

Pang, B. and Lee, L. (2005). Seeing stars: Exploiting class relationships for sentiment categorization with respect to rating scales. In *Proceedings of the 43rd Annual Meeting of the Association for Computational Linguistics (ACL'05)*, pages 115–124, Ann Arbor, Michigan, June. Association for Computational Linguistics.

Peters, M., Neumann, M., Iyyer, M., Gardner, M., Clark, C., Lee, K., and Zettlemoyer, L. (2018). Deep contextualized word representations. In *Proceedings of the 2018 Conference of the North American Chapter of the Association for Computational Linguistics: Human Language Technologies, Volume 1 (Long Papers)*, pages 2227–2237, New Orleans, Louisiana, June. Association for Computational Linguistics.

Peters, M. E., Ruder, S., and Smith, N. A. (2019). To tune or not to tune? adapting pretrained representations to diverse tasks. In *Proceedings of the 4th Workshop on Representation Learning for NLP (RepL4NLP-2019)*, pages 7–14, Florence, Italy, August. Association for Computational Linguistics.

Radford, A., Wu, J., Child, R., Luan, D., Amodei, D., and Sutskever, I. (2019). Language models are unsupervised multitask learners. Technical report, Open AI.

Radford, B. (2019). Multitask models for supervised protest detection in texts. *In Working Notes of CLEF 2019 - Conference and Labs of the Evaluation Forum*, 07.

Safaya, A. (2019). Event sentence detection task using attention model. *In Working Notes of CLEF 2019 - Conference and Labs of the Evaluation Forum*, 07.

Sanh, V., Debut, L., Chaumond, J., and Wolf, T. (2019). Distilbert, a distilled version of bert: smaller, faster, cheaper and lighter. In *NeurIPS EMC*^{2}$Workshop$.

Sun, C., Qiu, X., Xu, Y., and Huang, X. (2019). How to fine-tune bert for text classification? In Maosong Sun, et al., editors, *Chinese Computational Linguistics*, pages 194–206, Cham. Springer International Publishing.

Tenney, I., Xia, P., Chen, B., Wang, A., Poliak, A., McCoy, R. T., Kim, N., Durme, B. V., Bowman, S. R., Das, D., and Pavlick, E. (2019). What do you learn from context? probing for sentence structure in contextualized word representations. In *International Conference on Learning Representations*.

Wu, Y., Schuster, M., Chen, Z., Le, Q. V., Norouzi, M., Macherey, W., Krikun, M., Cao, Y., Gao, Q., Macherey, K., Klingner, J., Shah, A., Johnson, M., Liu, X., Łukasz Kaiser, Gouws, S., Kato, Y., Kudo, T., Kazawa, H., Stevens, K., Kurian, G., Patil, N., Wang, W., Young, C., Smith, J., Riesa, J., Rudnick, A., Vinyals, O., Corrado, G., Hughes, M., and Dean, J. (2016). Google's neural machine translation system: Bridging the gap between human and machine translation. *CoRR*, abs/1609.08144.

Yeh, A. (2000). More accurate tests for the statistical significance of result differences. In *Proceedings of the 18th Conference on Computational Linguistics - Volume 2*, COLING '00, pages 947–953, Stroudsburg, PA, USA. Association for Computational Linguistics.

Zhao, H., Lu, Z., and Poupart, P. (2015). Self-adaptive hierarchical sentence model. In *Proceedings of the 24th International Conference on Artificial Intelligence*, IJCAI'15, pages 4069–4076. AAAI Press.

Zhu, Y., Kiros, R., Zemel, R., Salakhutdinov, R., Urtasun, R., Torralba, A., and Fidler, S. (2015). Aligning books and movies: Towards story-like visual explanations by watching movies and reading books. In *The IEEE International Conference on Computer Vision (ICCV)*, December.

Proceedings of AESPEN 2020, pages 19–25
Language Resources and Evaluation Conference (LREC 2020), Marseille, 11–16 May 2020

Text Categorization for Conflict Event Annotation

Fredrik Olsson, Magnus Sahlgren, Fehmi Ben Abdesslem, Ariel Ekgren, Kristine Eck
RISE. Uppsala University
Intelligent Systems. Department of Peace and Conflict Research
Box 1263, 164 29 Kista, Sweden. Box 514, 751 20 Uppsala, Sweden
{fredrik.olsson, magnus.sahlgren, fehmi.ben.abdesslem, ariel.ekgren}@ri.se, kristine.eck@pcr.uu.se

Abstract

We cast the problem of event annotation as one of text categorization, and compare state of the art text categorization techniques on event data produced within the Uppsala Conflict Data Program (UCDP). Annotating a single text involves assigning the labels pertaining to at least 17 distinct categorization tasks, e.g., who were the attacking organization, who was attacked, and where did the event take place. The text categorization techniques under scrutiny are a classical Bag-of-Words approach; character-based contextualized embeddings produced by ELMo; embeddings produced by the BERT base model, and a version of BERT base fine-tuned on UCDP data; and a pre-trained and fine-tuned classifier based on ULMFiT. The categorization tasks are very diverse in terms of the number of classes to predict as well as the skewness of the distribution of classes. The categorization results exhibit a large variability across tasks, ranging from 30.3% to 99.8% F1-score.

Keywords: Event detection, Text categorization, Language models

1. Introduction

This study concerns the application of automatic text categorization techniques for the purpose of conflict event annotation using the data of the Uppsala Conflict Data Program.[1] In the terminology of UCDP, an event is an instance of fatal organized violence, defined by Sundberg and Melander (2013) as:

> The incidence of the use of armed force by an organized actor against another organized actor, or against civilians, resulting in at least 1 direct death in either the best, low or high estimate categories at a specific location and for a specific temporal duration

The present study seeks to investigate the automation of event annotation by taking advantage of recent advances in representation and transfer learning to harness the power of pre-trained and fine-tuned language models for representing the textual data subject to categorization. The purpose is to assess the relative performance of text categorization when the learner has access to language knowledge beyond that which is present in the training corpus, across a multitude of categorization tasks.

2. Related work

Document categorization, or document classification, consists in assigning one or several pre-defined labels, based on the contents of a whole document (here, a news article). In its simplest form, document categorization does not require that the ordering of tokens (or even the structures in which the tokens are arranged) is retained while extracting information. To the best of our knowledge, such document categorization introduced in this paper has not previously been applied to news articles for the purpose of event coding. Instead, however, sequence classification has been the focus of several works to automate the event encoding from news articles. Sequence classification is first based on the extraction of information, that is then used for attributing the characteristics of an event (such as the dyad[2] or the number of deaths) described in a document. Information extraction is typically based on classification tasks in which each unit (character, character sequence or token) in a text is classified as to whether it refers to a named entity (actors, location), time, number of casualties, or any other event characteristics.

In particular, there are several projects aiming at automating political event coding with sequence classification. The KEDS (Kansas Event Data System) project (Schrodt et al., 1994) was one of the first attempts, and was mainly based on parsing text to extract words that are pre-defined in dictionaries (actors and verbs).

TABARI (Schrodt, 2009) replaced KEDS by introducing significant improvements such as recognizing passive-voice sentences or disambiguating verbs that can also be nouns (e.g., Attack). TABARI was then replaced by Petrarch (Norris et al., 2017) and Universal Petrarch.

Petrarch stands for "Python Engine for Text Resolution And Related Coding Hierarchy". As its aforementioned predecessors, it is also a processing tool for machine-coding text describing events (i.e. news articles). It is designed to process fully-parsed news summaries, from which "whom-did-what-to-whom" relations are extracted. The output is then a dyad and an action. Date and location are also extracted. Petrarch is typically used by running the Phoenix pipeline,[3] which mainly consists in the following steps:

1. Extract articles and corresponding date from online sources using a web scraper[4].

2. Encode the sentences with Named Entity Recognition (NER) using Stanford CoreNLP (Manning et al.,

[1] https://ucdp.uu.se

[2] "A dyad is made up of two armed and opposing actors." See: https://www.pcr.uu.se/research/ucdp/definitions/

[3] https://phoenix-pipeline.readthedocs.io/

[4] https://github.com/openeventdata/scraper

2014)

3. Encode each sentence with [source_actor, action, and target_actor] (who does what to whom) using Petrarch.
4. Encode each sentence with a location using CLIFF-CALVIN (D'Ignazio et al., 2014) or Mordecai (Halterman, 2017).

In all these tools, actors and actions (verbs) are pre-defined in a specific ontology. Both Petrarch and Universal Petrarch use the same ontology for actors and verbs, based on TABARI dictionaries. TABARI dictionaries follow the CAMEO (Conflict and Mediation Event Observations) framework (Schrodt et al., 2008), which was initially intended as an extension of an ontology from the 60-70s called WEIS (McClelland, 2006). Another old ontology is COPDAB (Azar, 1980) in the 1980s. Competing modern ontologies to CAMEO are the IDEA (Bond et al., 2003) ontology from the 2000s, and the JRC-names (Ehrmann et al., 2017) in the 2010s, developed as a by-product of the EMM (European Media Monitor) project.

Currently, CAMEO is being replaced by PLOVER,[5] a new ontology with coverage of some new actions, vastly simplified coding of other actions, and a more flexible system for extensions and modifications.

Coding systems such as Petrarch and Universal Petrarch are rule-based: they use rules to decide which noun phrases are actors and which verb phrases are actions, and then compare these chunks of text against lists of hand-defined rules for coding actions and actors. Despite using NLP methods (e.g., NER), they are rarely using advanced machine learning algorithms. Among the few works using machine learning we can cite the work of Beieler (2016), who uses a character-based convolutional neural network, based on the work of Zhang et al. (2015), to determine the type of event action. However, the event actors are still determined with Petrarch, and the training dataset is also labelled with Petrarch.

Recently, categorizing news articles has also been experimented by Adhikari et al. (Adhikari et al., 2019) using BERT (introduced in Section 5.4.) to extract the topic of the articles.

3. Event annotation at UCDP

The Uppsala Conflict Data Program is the oldest ongoing data collection project for civil war, dating back almost 40 years. UCDP continuously updates its online database on armed conflicts and organized violence, in which information on several aspects of armed conflict such as conflict dynamics and conflict resolution is available. The database offers a web-based system for visualizing, handling and downloading data, including ready-made datasets on organized violence and peacemaking, all free of charge. UCDP is staffed by permanent full-time employees, handling data collection and processing detailed in (Högblad, 2019), including analysis and management.

The typical work-flow for a UCDP event annotator amounts to the following. For retrieving the news data from their data provider, an annotator:

1. inputs search terms to search selected news sources, then;
2. judges whether each news item retrieved:
   (a) describes a conflict event relevant to UCDP, and
   (b) either describes a new event, or brings new information about a known event.

Once a news text passes the above criteria, i.e., it is in fact relevant and contributes new information, the annotator looks for the following information in it:

- Geography (country, region, and even finer grained geographical reference points).
- Participants in the dyad.
- The number of deaths reported.
- Date or time period of the event.

More often than not, multiple news items relating to the same event are required in order to decide on all of the aforementioned attributes for an event. UCDP staff processes approximately 50 000 news items and other reports yearly, depending on the conflict situation in the world. In total, each text is manually annotated with up to 19 different labels.

The textual data in the UDCP database is annotated at the document level, rather than with in-text annotations at the sentence level. For instance, a document annotated with information about the dyad being part of an event exhibits an association between the dyad identifier and the document, but it does not provide information as to where in the document the reference to the dyad is located, and thus not how the surface form of the reference is manifested. This is a consequence of how the UCDP staff work when annotating event data, and it renders it natural to cast the event annotation problem as one of text categorization, rather than as a sequence extraction and labelling task. The annotation tasks consist in identifying the labels present in Table 1.

4. The dataset

The dataset at hand in this study consists of a combination of two distinct sources; the internal UCDP database compiled while UCDP annotators are working with identifying events in news text and reports, and the externally published Georeferenced Event Dataset (Sundberg and Melander, 2013). The former contains textual information related to the source documents read by the annotator while annotating the event, while the externally published event data is a clean, quantitative view of the text data. The combination of the data sources constitutes the ground truth, that the machine learning experiments carried out in this study will try to re-create.

4.1. The training set

The dataset used in the following experimental setup consists of 31 772 UCDP events, each of which is associated with a unique body of text in English. A body of text can consist of a (mix of) notes made by the annotator, records

[5] https://github.com/openeventdata/PLOVER

Label	Description	Number of classes	Class entropy
side_a	Name of state or government side involved.	299	3.9
side_b	Name of other participant.	301	3.5
dyad_name	Combination of side_a and side_b.	510	4.5
type_of_violence	State-based, non-state, or one sided.	3	0.8
conflict_name	The name of the conflict.	428	4.3
where_coordinates	Name of place of conflict.	4 125	7.4
region	Name of region.	5	1.4
country	Name of country.	84	3.2
adm_1	More precise name of region.	672	5.3
adm_2	Even more precise name of region.	1 739	6.5
deaths_a	Number of deaths reported for side_a.	75	1.4
deaths_b	Number of deaths reported for side_b.	115	1.9
deaths_civilians	Number of deaths reported for civilians.	117	1.5
deaths_unknown	Number of deaths reported for unknown side.	104	0.9
low	The lowest estimate of number of deaths reported for event.	175	3.2
best	The best estimate of number of deaths reported for event.	187	3.2
high	The highest estimate of number of deaths reported for event.	218	3.3

Table 1: The labels to be identified by tasks, along with their short descriptions, their number of classes, and their class entropy for the dataset consisting of 31 772 events. The class entropy is a measure of the class imbalance for a task such that a low value indicate higher imbalance. The class entropy is elaborated on in Section 4.2..

copied verbatim from an online conflict tracker, part or the whole of one or several news items, or some other distinct unit of text taken from an online resource. The dataset has been pre-processed and chosen so as to make sure that each text has given rise to a unique UCDP event. That is, in the current dataset there is a one-to-one relation between a body of text and an event. Thus, all texts that have resulted in two or more UCDP events have been omitted. The rationale behind this decision is the following: if a machine cannot reproduce the accuracy of the human annotators when presented with an admittedly simplified scenario (i.e., expect no more than exactly one event per text), then it will not perform well in a more realistic setting either (i.e., expect an arbitrary number of events to be described in each text). Only if the results in the simpler scenario are satisfactory should the more complicated setting be addressed.

4.2. The labels to predict

There are at least 17 different categorization tasks that a UCDP annotator has to deal with for every single event (omitting the temporal categories, i.e., the starting and ending date of an event). The annotations of the event data provided by UCDP constitutes the ground truth, and is as such the target of the predictions in the experiments to follow. In other words, for each of the bodies of texts in the dataset, there are 17 labels to predict. Table 1 shows the possible number of different classes that are in play in each of the annotation tasks, as well as the normalized entropy among those labels. The normalized class entropy value η is defined as $\eta(X) = -\sum_{i=1}^{n} \frac{p(x_i)\ln(p(x_i))}{\ln(n)}$ where X is the set of n possible classes, and $p(x_i)$ is the observed fraction of values equal to the ith class. The entropy is indicative of the distribution of classes within a task. A low entropy value is a sign of a skewed distribution, e.g., one class is significantly more frequent than the others, while a high entropy implies a more even distribution of classes. Combined, the size of the data, the number of classes and the class entropy tells us something about the expected complexity of the annotation task. For example, given the values in Table 1, it is expected that the task where_coordinates will be hard since it contains many classes (4 125) that are relatively evenly distributed across the dataset (the entropy value is high) giving, on average, relatively few events per class (31 722/4 125) to learn from. On the other hand, the task type_of_violence task exhibits a number of classes and class entropy at the other end of the spectrum: it is comprised of few classes (3) that are unevenly distributed in terms of occurrences in the dataset (entropy 0.8). Thus, an annotator is expected to perform well for (the majority) classes in the task.

Of course, there is more than meets the eye when it comes to how well a classifier actually manages to perform than just the number of classes, and their relative distribution, but these numbers give a hint as to what to expect.

5. Experimental setup

The experiments carried out in this study involve learning from the contents of the texts described in Section 4.1. to predict the classes of each task described in Section 4.2.. There are 17 different tasks, each of which will be addressed using five different text categorization techniques, as well as a random guessing-based baseline performance estimation.

For each task, the baseline (Section 5.1.), Bag-of-Words (BoW, Section 5.2.), ELMo experiments (Section 5.3.), the two BERT versions (Section 5.4.) are based on 5-fold cross-validation, with test data size set to 20% of the total corpus. This means that the baseline, BoW, ELMo, and BERT results are supported by approximately 30 000 data points each. Due to the time it took to complete the ULMFiT experiments (Section 5.5.), they are based on a single training and testing set, where the testing set is made up of approximately 6 000 data points, instead of the 5-fold cross-validation scheme employed in the other experiments. The split into training and testing data used by ULMFiT corresponds to the first fold in the baseline, BoW, ELMo and BERT cases, as it is made with the same logic and settings.

5.1. Baseline

A "dummy" classifier that guesses the class of a text by randomly drawing a class label from the class label distribution is used to assess a baseline upon which the machine learning-based classifiers should improve. The dummy classifier is available in scikit learn described by Pedregosa et al. (2011).

5.2. Using a standard Bag-of-Words approach

A classical way to represent documents in text categorization is as a collection of words, in which the order of the words is assumed to be irrelevant. This type of representation is usually referred to as Bag-of-Words. The assumption is naïve, but historically, it has produced relatively competitive results. The BoW representation used in the current setup contains single words (unigrams), as well as all combinations of two consecutive words in the training corpus (bigrams). A linear learning method (Logistic Regression) is then used to train classifiers to distinguish between the classes in the different tasks.

The BoW approach is included in the experiments since it, in the past, has been a go-to solution in many text categorization tasks and thus constitutes a sensible baseline that more modern approaches should beat.

5.3. ELMo

Embeddings from Language Models (ELMo) described by (Peters et al., 2018), is a deep character-based neural network that learns embeddings by predicting the next token given an input sequence. The network architecture includes both convolutional and (bidirectional) LSTM layers, and produces an embedding that that is sensitive to the particular context of the input sequence. Contextualized embeddings have proven to be highly beneficial when using the embeddings as representation in downstream natural language processing tasks such as categorization, entity recognition, and question answering. In the current setup, an existing pretrained version[6] of ELMo is used to produce a single 1 024 elements long feature vector for the body of text associated to each event in the UCDP data. The data used for pretraining the ELMo model used here is reported to be approximately 20 million randomly selected texts from Wikipedia and CommonCrawl, amounting to a total training time of 3 days per language. The ELMo feature vectors are then used as input to a non-linear learner (Random Forest) to train a classifier for distinguishing between the classes in each of the 17 tasks.

The ELMo approach is included in the experiments since it has proven to be a simple and effective way of incorporating language knowledge in machine learning situations where training data is scarce.

[6] `https://github.com/HIT-SCIR/ELMoForManyLangs`

5.4. BERT

Bidirectional Encoder Representations from Transformers (BERT) (Devlin et al., 2019) is a deep, attention-based neural network architecture that produces a contextualized representation of a text by taking both the left and right context into account simultaneously. In this respect, it differs from ELMo, which builds its representation of text based on a concatenating representations from the left and right context. Since its inception, BERT has been shown to improve the state-of-the art on many language processing tasks, including some text categorization ones.

In the experiments to follow, we use two versions of BERT: the original large pre-trained uncased base model made available via Hugging Face's Transformers (Wolf et al., 2019), and a version of the same model fine-tuned on the UCDP data.

5.5. ULMFiT

Universal Language Modelling Fine-Tuning (ULMFiT), described in (Howard and Ruder, 2018), is a three step method for transferring general language use to specific categorization tasks. The method consists of the following three steps:

1. Train a language model on an unannotated corpus of general language.
2. Fine-tune the language model based on unannotated in-domain texts.
3. Train and fine-tune a text classifier on annotated texts.

An initial language model (Step 1) is readily available online. ULMFiT is pretrained on a subset of the English Wikipedia containing more than 103 million running words taken from more than 28 000 verified *Good* or *Featured* articles (Merity et al., 2016). In Step 2, we used the texts associated with the 31 722 UCDP events to fine-tune the language model. Finally, in Step 3, a classifier was created for each of the 17 different tasks outlined in Table 1.

The implementation of ULMFiT used in the current experiment is based on the AWD-LSTM language model architecture described by (Merity et al., 2017).

The ULMFiT approach is included in the experiments because it is a robust method for leveraging the language knowledge of a pretrained model and its ability to adjust that model based on in-domain data, without requiring vast computational resources. Until recently, ULMFiT produced state-of-the art classifiers for a number of benchmarks.

6. Categorization results

Table 2 on the next page shows the results from the experiments in terms F1-score for the random baseline, the BoW-based Logistic Regression classifier, the ELMo-based Random Forest classifier, the original and fine-tuned BERT-based Random Forest classifiers, as well as for ULMFiT. As an example, refer back to the discussion of the complexity of the annotation tasks in terms of the number of classes and the class entropy in Section 4.2., and consider the baseline F1-score result for the task type_of_violence

Table 2: UCDP document categorization results.

Task	Cls	En	B.F	BW.F	E.F	BE.F	BF.F	U.F
side_a	299	3.9	5.0	76.8	76.2	81.1	84.9	84.7
side_b	301	3.5	8.1	73.7	75.5	78.3	82.0	82.5
dyad_name	510	4.5	4.1	66.9	72.5	75.6	79.3	80.8
type_of_violence	3	0.8	56.6	88.8	85.8	88.6	89.6	91.8
conflict_name	428	4.3	4.2	69.5	73.4	76.9	80.7	82.7
where_coordinates	4125	7.4	0.3					30.3
region	5	1.4	28.7	99.4	89.6	97.7	98.7	99.8
country	84	3.2	6.9	95.5	82.8	90.2	94.7	97.4
adm_1	672	5.3	1.0	64.2	62.2	62.8	65.1	77.7
adm_2	1739	6.5	0.4	27.5				41.3
deaths_a	75	1.4	46.8	63.6	83.1	82.2	82.2	73.3
deaths_b	115	1.9	35.6	59.0	75.1	74.8	75.5	67.4
deaths_civilians	117	1.5	48.7	63.8	84.1	83.5	83.7	70.9
deaths_unknown	104	0.9	72.5	79.0	93.3	92.7	92.7	80.8
low	175	3.2	8.5	32.3	61.6	58.5	58.5	37.9
best	187	3.2	8.3	32.6	61.1	58.1	58.4	41.6
high	218	3.3	8.5	32.4	61.8	58.6	58.7	40.0

Task	The name of the annotation task.
Cls	The number of distinct classes for a particular task.
En	The class entropy: a high value corresponds to a more evenly distribution of instances per class.
B	Baseline, random guessing based on distribution of labels.
BW	Bag of words representation.
E	ELMo representations + non-linear classifier.
BE	BERT representations + non-linear classifier.
BF	BERT representations, model fine-tuned on UCDP data + non-linear classifier.
U	ULMFiT pretrained on Wikipedia, fine-tuned and trained on UCDP data.
F	weighted F1-score.
	Light grey cells in the table indicate a failure of the classifier to complete the corresponding task. The failures are due to the size of the models: for tasks with many classes, the memory consumption of the learner exceeds that of the available memory (which in this case is 255Gb).

which is given in column B.F in Table 2. The task concerns only three highly imbalanced classes, which in effect means it is easy to get a fairly good score just by making a vaguely informed guess with respect to the class. The random guessing-based baseline F1-score is 56.6%. All trained classifiers improve on the baseline, with ULMFiT performing the best at an F1-score of 91.8%, a 35.2 percent point improvement.

The other example in Section 4.2. is that of where_coordinates. The baseline results for the task align with the expected outcome given the size of the data, the number of classes, and the class entropy: the F1-score value is low, at around 0.3% of a possible 100%. The ULMFiT classifier improves the F1-score given the baseline with 30.0%. Still, at an F1-score of 30.3%, the classifier clearly underperforms vis-à-vis the human annotated data.

According to Table 2, the tasks that the hardest for the classifiers are:

- where_coordinates (ULMFiT F1-score: 30.3%)
- adm_2 (ULMFiT F1-score: 41.3%)
- low (ELMo F1-score: 61.6%)
- best (ELMo F1-score: 61.1%)
- high (ELMo F1-score: 61.8%)

The above are all tasks in which there are many classes, and thus little data to learn from per class. The following are the tasks on which the classifiers performed the best:

- region (ULMFiT F1-score: 99.8%)
- country (ULMFiT F1-score: 97.4%)
- deaths_unknown (ELMo F1-score: 93.3%)
- type_of_violence (ULMFiT F1-score: 91.8%)
- side_a (BERT fine-tuned F1-score: 84.9%)
- deaths_civilians (ELMo F1-score: 84.1%)
- deaths_a (ELMo F1-score: 83.1%)
- conflict_name (ULMFiT F1-score: 82.7%)
- side_b (ULMFiT F1-score: 82.5%)
- dyad_name (ULMFiT F1-score: 80.8%)

However, it should be emphasized that the experimental setting in this report is a simplified one that only includes data in which each textual body corresponds to exactly one UCDP event.

7. Discussion

From the results of this study, we make two observations. The first observation concerns text categorization for event annotation, while the other is about the developments in the field of transfer learning in NLP.

7.1. Text categorization for event annotation

By casting the event annotation problem as one of text categorization, we have gained initial insight into the complexity of assigning values to the individual attributes of events. Some attributes are naturally harder to automatically predict than others: for instance, the finer-grained geographical location of an event (where_coordinates) is harder to assess than the immediately broader region (country). Similarly, the dyad name is harder to predict than the names of its participants. It is also clear that automated text categorization has value in that it performs very near the level of human annotators, for some tasks. This begs the question: How can we best make use of text categorization for the purpose of improving the human annotation process in terms of, e.g., speed, and consistency? We believe that the categorization results reported in this study are encouraging enough to warrant continued investigations with respect to its use in the manual annotation process, as well as further improvements of the categorization results. As for the latter, there are two immediate issues that require attention. The first issue is to go from the simplified setting of the current experiments to one that allows the more natural many-to-many relationship between texts and events. The second issue is to investigate methods for making use of the conditional dependencies between tasks e.g., that certain dyads are active only in certain geographical locations.

7.2. Transfer learning in NLP

Although the bag-of-words approach is a strong baseline, it is almost always better to utilize pre-training and fine-tuning on domain-specific data. ELMo and the original BERT model are both pre-trained on large amounts of data, and do not make use of any in-domain data in the current setting. Still, both models perform well, beating the BoW baseline in most cases. Furthermore, fine-tuning pre-trained models on domain-specific data always helps: the fine-tuned BERT model beats the original model across all tasks.

Acknowledgements

The study presented in this paper is funded by Riksbankens Jubileumsfond, via the research project *Automation of the Uppsala Conflict Data Program (UCDP)*, reference number IN18-0710:1.

The authors wish to thank the anonymous reviewers for valuable and thoughtful comments.

8. Bibliographical References

Adhikari, A., Ram, A., Tang, R., and Lin, J. (2019). Docbert: Bert for document classification. *ArXiv*, abs/1904.08398.

Azar, E. E. (1980). The conflict and peace data bank (COPDAB) project. *Journal of Conflict Resolution*, 24(1):143–152.

Beieler, J. (2016). Generating politically-relevant event data. *arXiv preprint arXiv:1609.06239*.

Bond, D., Bond, J., Oh, C., Jenkins, J. C., and Taylor, C. L. (2003). Integrated data for events analysis (IDEA): An event typology for automated events data development. *Journal of Peace Research*, 40(6):733–745.

Devlin, J., Chang, M.-W., Lee, K., and Toutanova, K. (2019). BERT: Pre-training of deep bidirectional transformers for language understanding. In *Proceedings of the 2019 Conference of the North American Chapter of the Association for Computational Linguistics: Human Language Technologies, Volume 1 (Long and Short Papers)*, pages 4171–4186, Minneapolis, Minnesota, June. Association for Computational Linguistics.

D'Ignazio, C., Bhargava, R., Zuckerman, E., and Beck, L. (2014). Cliff-clavin: Determining geographic focus for news. *News KDD: Data Science for News Publishing*, 2014.

Ehrmann, M., Jacquet, G., and Steinberger, R. (2017). Jrc-names: Multilingual entity name variants and titles as linked data. *Semantic Web*, 8(2):283–295.

Halterman, A. (2017). Mordecai: Full text geoparsing and event geocoding. *The Journal of Open Source Software*, 2(9).

Högblad, S. (2019). UCDP GED Codebook version 19.1.

Howard, J. and Ruder, S. (2018). Universal language model fine-tuning for text classification. In *Proceedings of the 56th Annual Meeting of the Association for Computational Linguistics (Volume 1: Long Papers)*, pages 328–339.

Manning, C. D., Surdeanu, M., Bauer, J., Finkel, J., Bethard, S. J., and McClosky, D. (2014). The Stanford CoreNLP natural language processing toolkit. In *Association for Computational Linguistics (ACL) System Demonstrations*, pages 55–60.

McClelland, C. (2006). World Event/Interaction Survey (WEIS) Project, 1966-1978.

Merity, S., Xiong, C., Bradbury, J., and Socher, R. (2016). Pointer sentinel mixture models. *arXiv preprint arXiv:1609.07843*.

Merity, S., Keskar, N. S., and Socher, R. (2017). Regularizing and optimizing lstm language models. *arXiv preprint arXiv:1708.02182*.

Norris, C., Schrodt, P., and Beieler, J. (2017). PETRARCH2: Another event coding program. *The Journal of Open Source Software*, 2(9), 1.

Pedregosa, F., Varoquaux, G., Gramfort, A., Michel, V., Thirion, B., Grisel, O., Blondel, M., Prettenhofer, P., Weiss, R., Dubourg, V., Vanderplas, J., Passos, A., Cournapeau, D., Brucher, M., Perrot, M., and Duchesnay, E. (2011). Scikit-learn: Machine learning in Python. *Journal of Machine Learning Research*, 12:2825–2830.

Peters, M., Neumann, M., Iyyer, M., Gardner, M., Clark, C., Lee, K., and Zettlemoyer, L. (2018). Deep contextualized word representations. In *Proceedings of the 2018 Conference of the North American Chapter of the Association for Computational Linguistics: Human Language Technologies, Volume 1 (Long Papers)*, pages 2227–2237.

Schrodt, P. A., Davis, S. G., and Weddle, J. L. (1994). Political Science: KEDS - A Program for the Machine Coding of Event Data. *Social Science Computer Review*, 12(4):561–587.

Schrodt, P. A., Yilmaz, O., Gerner, D. J., and Hermreck, D. (2008). The CAMEO (conflict and mediation event observations) actor coding framework. In *2008 Annual Meeting of the International Studies Association*.

Schrodt, P. A. (2009). Tabari: Textual analysis by augmented replacement instructions. *Dept. of Political Science, University of Kansas, Blake Hall, Version 0.7. 3B3*, pages 1–137.

Sundberg, R. and Melander, E. (2013). Introducing the ucdp georeferenced event dataset. *Journal of Peace Research*, 50(4):523–532.

Wolf, T., Debut, L., Sanh, V., Chaumond, J., Delangue, C., Moi, A., Cistac, P., Rault, T., Louf, R., Funtowicz, M., and Brew, J. (2019). Huggingface's transformers: State-of-the-art natural language processing. *ArXiv*, abs/1910.03771.

Zhang, X., Zhao, J., and LeCun, Y. (2015). Character-level convolutional networks for text classification. In *Advances in neural information processing systems*, pages 649–657.

Proceedings of AESPEN 2020, pages 26–34
Language Resources and Evaluation Conference (LREC 2020), Marseille, 11–16 May 2020

TF-IDF Character *N*-grams versus Word Embedding-based Models for Fine-grained Event Classification: A Preliminary study

Jakub Piskorski, Guillaume Jacquet
Polish Academy of Sciences, Joint Research Centre - European Commission
jpiskorski@gmail.com, guillaume.jacquet@ec.europa.eu

Abstract

Automating the detection of event mentions in online texts and their classification vis-a-vis domain-specific event type taxonomies has been acknowledged by many organisations worldwide to be of paramount importance in order to facilitate the process of intelligence gathering. This paper reports on some preliminary experiments of comparing various linguistically-lightweight approaches for fine-grained event classification based on short text snippets reporting on events. In particular, we compare the performance of a TF-IDF-weighted character *n*-gram SVM-based model with SVMs trained on various off-the-shelf pre-trained word embeddings (GLOVE, BERT, FASTTEXT) as features. We exploit a relatively large event corpus consisting of circa 610K short text event descriptions classified using 25-event categories that cover political violence and protest events. The best results, i.e., 83.5% macro and 92.4% micro F_1 score, were obtained using the TF-IDF-weighted character *n*-gram model.

Keywords: event classification, machine learning, word embeddings, subword models

1. Introduction

Recently various organisations around the world have acknowledged the paramount importance of exploiting the ever-growing amount of information published on the web on various types of events for early detection of threats, carrying out risk analysis and predicting future developments (King and Lowe, 2003; Yangarber et al., 2008; Atkinson et al., 2011; Piskorski et al., 2011; Leetaru and Schrodt, 2013; Ward et al., 2013; Pastor-Galindo et al., 2020). Since a clear majority of information on relevant events is provided in the form of free text (e.g. news articles), an important task is to automatically detect mentions of events of interest in such texts and to classify them using domain specific taxonomies.

This paper reports on a preliminary study of exploiting linguistically-lightweight approaches for fine-grained event classification for short texts reporting on events. In particular, we compare the performance of various SVM-based classifiers, including a TF-IDF-weighted character *n*-gram model with various models that exploit off-the-shelf pre-trained word embeddings (GLOVE, BERT and FASTTEXT) as features.

Our research has two aims. Firstly, we are interested to develop a robust, fine-grained, event classifier that can be: (a) easily ported across languages, (b) quickly adapted to new domains/event taxonomies, and (c) applied to classify events based solely on short text snippets. The decision to focus on classification from short texts come from the type of incomplete event data that is often at hand, e.g. historical news event information stored in so called event templates, that apart from automatically extracted meta-data include only the title and 1-2 initial sentences from a news article from which the event information was extracted (Atkinson et al., 2017). Secondly, we are interested to gain a better understanding of the amount of data that is required to obtain 'acceptable' classification performance in order to better estimate the effort required for new classification-scheme development cycles.

The main contributions of the work reported in this paper can be summarized as follows:

- we make available a clean and tuned version of a large corpus of circa 600K short text snippets tagged with fine-grained event category labels (mainly covering political violence and protest events) for event classification experiments, which was derived from a manually-curated event repository created by human experts in the context of the ACLED[1]
- we report on the comparison of the performance of various SVM-based classifiers, including a TF.IDF-weighted character *n*-gram model and models that exploit various pre-trained word embeddings as features, evaluated on the aforementioned event corpus.

We are not aware of any similar study on automated event classification in terms of the size of the underlying training-test dataset and fine-grained event categories. Furthermore, given the specific nature of the dataset exploited, i.e. text snippets resembling news headlines and initial sentences in news articles, we believe that the reported results constitute a good approximation for the to-be-expected performance when applying the same methods on real news-article corpora.

The rest of the paper is structured as follows. First, Section 2. provides an overview of related work. Next, Section 3. describes the dataset used for carrying out the experiments. Subsequently, Section 4. presents the results of the performance of the various classification models explored. Finally, Section 5. gives conclusions and an outlook on future work.

2. Related Work

The research and progress on the task of identifying event mentions in text documents and classification of these

[1] `https://www.acleddata.com` initiative, and

events was initially driven by the Message Understanding Contests (Sundheim, 1991; Chinchor, 1998) and the Automatic Content Extraction (ACE) Challenges (Doddington et al., 2004; LDC, 2008). In particular, many approaches to event detection and classification have been reported and evaluated on the event corpora (ca. 6000 event mentions in ca. 500 documents) developed in the context of the aforementioned ACE Challenges, which range from shallow (Liao and Grishman, 2010; Hong et al., 2011) to deep machine learning approaches (Nguyen and Grishman, 2015; Nguyen et al., 2016).

Recently, the Multi-lingual Event Detection and Coreference task has been introduced as part of the Text Analysis Conference (TAC) in 2016[2] and 2017[3], which included an Event Nugget Detection subtask, focusing on detection and classification of intra-document event mention types and subtypes with 9 and 38 categories respectively, that cover events from various domains (e.g., finances and jurisdiction). The related evaluation datasets are rather tiny, i.e., ca. 500 documents with less than 10K labelled event mentions.

Furthermore, a CLEF ProtestNews Track was organized recently (Hürriyetoğlu et al., 2019) with three shared tasks aimed at identifying and extracting event information from news articles across multiple countries, where one of the tasks explicitly focused on classification of the news articles into "protests" versus "non protests" depending on whether the article reports on protests, and a more fine-grained binary classification task that focused on labelling sentences that refer to reporting on protest events. Similarly to the TAC tasks, the evaluation datasets are rather small (4K news articles, and 6K labelled sentences). In particular, approaches exploiting word embeddings to tackle these tasks have been reported (Ollagnier and Williams, 2019).

The work most similar to ours on event classification has been presented in (Nugent et al., 2017). This paper studies the performance of various models, including ones that exploit word embeddings as features, for detection and classification of natural disaster and critical socio-political events in news articles, based on analysing their initial sentences. However, the underlying event type taxonomy is relatively coarse-grained (7 types) and the size of the evaluation dataset is relatively small (ca. 2.5K documents).

In the work reported in this paper we only focus on the task of event classification, and given the specific dataset (in particular, its size) exploited for carrying out our, it is difficult to make direct comparisons with the shared tasks and evaluation campaigns mentioned above.

3. Datasets

For carrying out our research, we exploited the data gathered in the context of the Armed Conflict Location & Event Data Project (ACLED)[4]. ACLED (Raleigh et al., 2010) collects human-moderated records on the dates, actors, types of violence, locations, and fatalities of all reported political violence and protest events across Africa, some regions of Asia, the Middle East, and Southeastern and Eastern Europe and the Balkans. In particular, we exploited the manually curated data provided on the ACLED web page[5] and extracted from them event records consisting of: event type, event subtype and textual description, which mentions basic information on the event. ACLED uses an event ontology consisting of 6 main event types, which are subdivided into 25 more fine-grained subtypes, listed in Table 1. Two examples of event descriptions for `Abduction/forced disappearance` and `Peaceful protest` events resp. are given below.

```
[1] A girl was kidnapped in Ain El
    Turk, Oran by unidentified
    individuals. Police managed to
    free the girl 3 days later.

[2] On 20 February, a group of 30
    anarchists protested in front
    of the Russian consulate in
    north Athens unfurling banners
    in support of Russian anarchists
    and scattering fliers.
```

The detailed definition of the ACLED event hierarchy is presented in (ACLED, 2019). We were able to extract from ACLED curated resources 614107 event triples, consisting of the type, subtype and short event description. We will refer to this corpus as ACLED-O (ACLED Original). This corpus was subsequently cleaned, through: (a) removing from the event descriptions quotation and similar non-content relevant characters, (b) removing too obvious markers that would artificially help the classifier such as initial phrases in the event descriptions indicating the specific event type or subtype, e.g. "*Arrest:*", and (c) filtering out event triples that contain event descriptions consisting of less than 20 characters (considered as non informative). We will refer to the resulting corpus as ACLED-C (ACLED Clean). Finally, we created a third version of the corpus to check if the mention of geographical names in an event description could impact the results of the classifier. We replaced in ACLED-C the occurrences of geographical names with a generic location tag, using the GEONAMES[6] gazetteer. The resulting dataset will be referred to as ACLED-CG. The specific event type/subtypes and related statistics of the ACLED-C datasets are listed in Table 1.

The distribution of the length of event descriptions for the ACLED-C dataset is shown in Figure 1. We can observe that the length of the vast majority of the event descriptions is between 30 and 400 characters, which corresponds to the length of a title and 1-2 leading sentences in a news article reporting on an event. We have, however, observed some outliers with a length of more than 1000 characters.

[2]`https://tac.nist.gov//2016/KBP/Event/index.html`

[3]`https://tac.nist.gov/2017/KBP/Event/index.html`

[4]`https://www.acleddata.com`

[5]`https://www.acleddata.com/curated-data-files/`

[6]`https://www.geonames.org/`

Event Type	Event Subtype	Number	Percent.
BATTLES		151955	24.84%
	Armed clash	141871	23.19%
	Government regains territory	6119	1.00%
	Non-state actor overtakes territory	3965	0.65%
EXPLOSION AND REMOTE VIOLENCE		134153	21.93%
	Chemical weapon	106	0.02%
	Air/drone strike	46222	7.56%
	Suicide bomb	1775	0.29%
	Shelling/artillery/missile attack	52716	8.62%
	Remote explosive/landmine/IED	29514	4.83%
	Grenade	3820	0.62%
VIOLENCE AGAINST CIVILIANS		70844	11.58%
	Sexual violence	1770	0.29%
	Attack	63121	10.32%
	Abduction/forced disappearance	5953	0.97%
PROTESTS		177082	28.95%
	Peaceful protest	161829	26.46%
	Protest with intervention	12636	2.07%
	Excessive force against protesters	2617	0.43%
RIOTS		50545	8.26%
	Violent demonstration	27092	4.43%
	Mob violence	23453	3.83%
STRATEGIC DEVELOPMENTS		27099	4.43%
	Agreement	1415	0.23%
	Arrests	3518	0.58%
	Change to group/activity	6112	1.00%
	Disrupted weapons use	4641	0.76%
	Headquarters or base established	589	0.10%
	Looting/property destruction	6008	0.98%
	Non-violent transfer of territory	1821	0.30%
	Other	2995	0.49%
TOTAL		611678	

Table 1: ACLED-C event corpus statistics: Number and percentage of event types and subtypes.

4. Experiments

4.1. Classification Tasks

In our research we were primarily interested in the fine-grained event classification vis-a-vis the subtypes enumerated in Table 1, which we call **Event Subtype Classification**. For the sake of completeness, and given the availability of the corpora introduced in the previous Section we also evaluated the performance of coarse-grained event classification, which will be referred to as **Event Type Classification**, in line with the terminology introduced in the ACLED corpus. In particular, we compared the results obtained on all three versions of this corpus, i.e., (ACLED-O, ACLED-C and ACLED-CG).

4.2. Approaches

We compare two main approaches to the Event Subtype/Type Classification, both using Support Vector Machine (SVM) model, where one is based on TF-IDF character n-grams features, and the other on exploiting various word embeddings as features for training the models. The SVM classification is 'pairwise' (One-Versus-One; OVO), meaning that a binary classifier is trained for each pair of classes and the class which receives most votes (highest count) is selected. This method of multi-class classification was favoured over One-Versus-Rest classification due to overall better results obtained. We chose an SVM classification approach following its widely-acknowledged strong performance on text classification tasks (Joachims, 1998; Yang and Liu, 1999; Qin and Wang, 2009; Ye et al., 2009; Chesney et al., 2017).

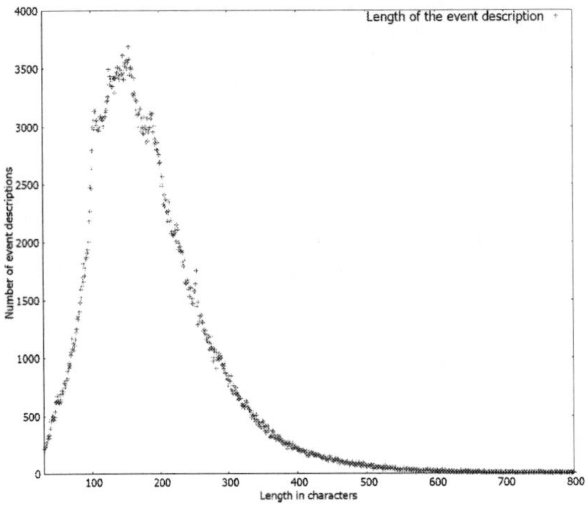

Figure 1: The distribution of the length of event descriptions for ACLED-C dataset.

4.2.1. TF-IDF character n-gram approach

We follow a bag-of-words (BoW) model for extracting TF-IDF features from the character n-grams contained within each event description. We use an n-gram range between 3 and 5-grams. We exclude the n-grams occurring in less than 5 event descriptions. We observed during our experiments that these parameters could be slightly modified without important impact on the classification results. The vectorisation is implemented with L2 normalisation, in order to normalise for the number of expressions in each class, and sublinear TF calculations (which log-scales the TF counts). In contrast to the word embedding approaches described in the next section, here the dimensionality of the TF-IDF vectors varies depending on the training set size, and each event description is represented by a large sparse vector instead of the short full vector used in the word embedding representation. In the presented experiments, the TF-IDF vectors varied from 26 705, when using 0.5% of the training set, to 365 175 when using the full training set.

4.2.2. Word embedding-based approach

Word embeddings have proved to be an efficient method for solving various natural language processing tasks in recent years, enabling, in particular, various machine learning models that rely on vector representation as input to enjoy richer representations of text input while alleviating high-dimensionality issues. Formally, a word embedding is a function $Words \rightarrow \mathbb{R}^d$ that maps words to real-valued vectors of a fixed dimension (Bengio et al., 2003). Many authors have reported that word embeddings perform surprisingly well for text classification tasks (Reimers and Gurevych, 2019). In our initial experiments we used the popular GLOVE, BERT and FASTTEXT embeddings.

GLOVE (Pennington et al., 2014) word embeddings are obtained through exploitation of aggregated global word-word co-occurrence statistics from a large corpus. For our experiments we used the pre-trained GLOVE 300-dimensional vectors trained on WIKIPEDIA and the English Gigaword corpus[7]. To compute a GLOVE embedding for an event description we averaged the single GLOVE embeddings of all words contained in the event description.

BERT (Devlin et al., 2019) is a pre-trained transformer network (Vaswani et al., 2017), which can be used to extract word and sentence embedding vectors for various NLP tasks. The main difference vis-a-vis the classical word embeddings like WORD2VEC is the fact that BERT produces word representations that are dynamically informed by the words around them. For our experiments we exploited the pre-trained BERT multilingual (104 languages) cased model[8] that produces 768-dimensional vectors. As with GLOVE, we averaged the single BERT embeddings for all words in each event description. We have chosen the averaging of the BERT vectors based on the relatively good results reported on 7 different classification tasks in (Reimers and Gurevych, 2019), which yielded on average almost identical results vis-a-vis exploiting the [CLS] special token output from a BERT transformer.

FASTTEXT embeddings (Mikolov et al., 2018) are based on a model where each word is represented as a bag of character n-grams, and the vector representing the word is constructed as the sum of the vectors for the character n-grams it consists of. In our experiments, we exploited the pre-trained 300-dimensional FASTTEXT vectors, trained on Common Crawl[9] and Wikipedia (Grave et al., 2018) using CBOW with position-weights with character n-grams of length 5, and a window of size 5.

4.3. Experiment settings

For implementing the SVM models, we use Scikit-learn (Pedregosa et al., 2011), the machine learning library for Python. The SVM pairwise classification is implemented using Scikit-learn's LinearSVC SVM classifier with the One-Versus-One wrapper (Pedregosa et al., 2011).

We use 10-fold shuffle-split cross-validation, split 75% training and 25% testing for all experiments. The general approach was as follows: the corpus is randomly shuffled (with a constant random state initialisation value for reproducibility) 10 times, and each shuffled version is then separated for training and testing. With this method, it is not guaranteed that each fold will be different, but it is likely with sizeable data sets; nonetheless, we favour this technique over k-fold cross-validation as it maximises the training data available, even for the smallest event subtypes.

4.4. Evaluation Methodology

For the sake of evaluating the event classification performance we used the classical precision, recall, and F_1 metrics, which are formally defined as follows:

$$Precision = \frac{TP}{TP + FP} \tag{1}$$

$$Recall = \frac{TP}{TP + FN} \tag{2}$$

[7] https://catalog.ldc.upenn.edu/LDC2011T07
[8] https://github.com/google-research/bert
[9] https://commoncrawl.org/

$$F_1 = \frac{2 \cdot Recall \cdot Precision}{Recall + Precision} \quad (3)$$

where TP, TN, FP and FN denote true positives, true negatives, false positives and false negatives respectively. To obtain a fine-grained picture, we evaluate both *micro* and *macro* versions of the introduced metrics and denote them with P_{mic}, P_{mac}, R_{mic}, R_{mac}, $F_{1_{mic}}$, $F_{1_{mac}}$ resp. While the micro versions calculate the performance from the individual true positives, true negatives, false positives, and false negatives of the 25-class model, in macro-averaging, one computes the performance of each individual class separately, and then an average of the obtained scores. In other words, micro versions of the metrics are indicators of the performance quality at the individual event level (biased by event type frequency), whereas the macro versions are indicators of the performance quality at the event type level disregarding the event type distribution.

4.5. Results

First, we evaluated the performance of the TF-IDF character *n*-gram based SVM on each of the three corpora, namely, ACLED-O, ACLED-C and ACLED-CG. The performance of the respective models is presented in Table 2. Given that there were no observable differences in performance on the three corpora, in particular between ACLED-C and ACLED-CG, all further experiments were carried out only on ACLED-C corpus.

Dataset	P_{mic}	R_{mic}	$F_{1_{mic}}$	P_{mac}	R_{mac}	$F_{1_{mac}}$
ACLED-O	0.924	0.924	0.924	0.884	0.816	0.845
ACLED-C	0.924	0.924	0.924	0.871	0.807	0.835
ACLED-CG	0.921	0.921	0.921	0.872	0.805	0.834

Table 2: Character *n*-gram-based SVM results on 75% of the ACLED-O, ACLED-C and ACLED-CG datasets

The micro and macro F_1 scores for the **Event Subtype Classification** task (fine grained classification) using different portions of the ACLED-C corpus for training and testing purposes $(0.5\%, 1\%, 5\%, 10\%, 50\%$ and $100\%)$ are presented in Figure 2. The corresponding macro precision and recall figures are compared in Figure 3. We can observe that:

- overall, the TF-IDF character *n*-gram based model performs better than word embedding-based models, except the case when less than ca. 3% of data (ca. 20K events) is available for training, in whose context GLOVE-based approach works better with respect to the macro F_1 score,
- in particular, with the full dataset available (600K events) the TF-IDF character *n*-gram based model (reaching max. of 83.5% macro and 92.4% micro F_1 score) clearly outperforms ($>$ 10%) the word embedding-based approaches,
- already with a very small portion of the data, i.e., 0.5% (ca. 3K events) one obtained fairly good micro F_1 scores, ranging from 71.8% to 77.4%, whereas obtaining macro F_1 scores above 60% requires at least 10 to 50% of the data (60-300K events) for the various word embedding-based models,
- in general, out of the three word embedding-based approaches, GLOVE appears to work best, although with availability of more data the differences between F_1 scores for all three word embedding-based approaches become smaller and converge.

The micro and macro F_1 scores for the **Event Type classification** task (coarse grained) using different portions of the ACLED-C corpus for training and testing purposes $(0.5\%, 1\%, 5\%, 10\%, 50\%$ and $100\%)$ are presented in Figure 4. In general, we can observe the same patterns as in the case of fine-grained event classification, i.e., TF-IDF character *n*-gram based model performs better (reaching max. 94.6% micro and 92.5% macro F_1 scores when using the entire corpus), GLOVE outperforming the other word embedding-based models with smaller amount of training data, etc. However, not surprisingly though, the main difference in this context are significantly higher micro and macro F_1 scores ranging from 78 to 85% and 68 to 77% resp. when training the models on a tiny portion of the data (i.e., 0.5% of the data, which corresponds to ca. 3K events). Similar results were obtained in the work reported in (Nugent et al., 2017) that compared the performance of similar-in-nature models trained and evaluated on comparable corpora in terms of its size.

4.6. Error Analysis

To get a better insight into the most frequent errors for the event subtype classification task we computed confusion matrices for the different approaches evaluated and concluded that the types of errors were similar across the different settings. Therefore, for the sake of completeness, we only present here the confusion matrix for the GLOVE-based SVM classifier, which is depicted in Figure 5.
We can observe from the confusion matrix that:

- classification of event subtypes within the `Explosions and Remote Violence` event type works best, i.e., true positive rate ranging from 82% to 95%,
- classification of event subtypes within the `Strategic Developments` and `Riots` main event types yields worst results on average, i.e., true positive rate ranging from 0.60% to 0.79%,
- most of the errors within the `Battles`, `Riots` and `Protests` main event types are due to mislabelling the event subtype with another subtype within the same main event type, which appears to be a logical consequence of small nuances of the definitions of the specific event subtypes and resulting high overlap of the respective vocabulary used in the event descriptions, e.g., `Government regains territory` versus `Non-state actor overtakes territory`

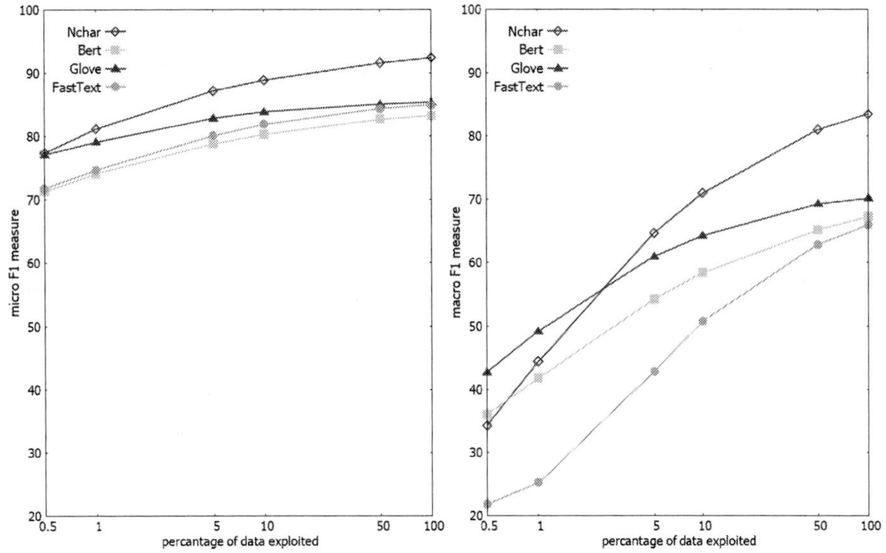

Figure 2: Micro and Macro F_1 measure results for Event Subtype Classification on the different subsets of ACLED-C dataset.

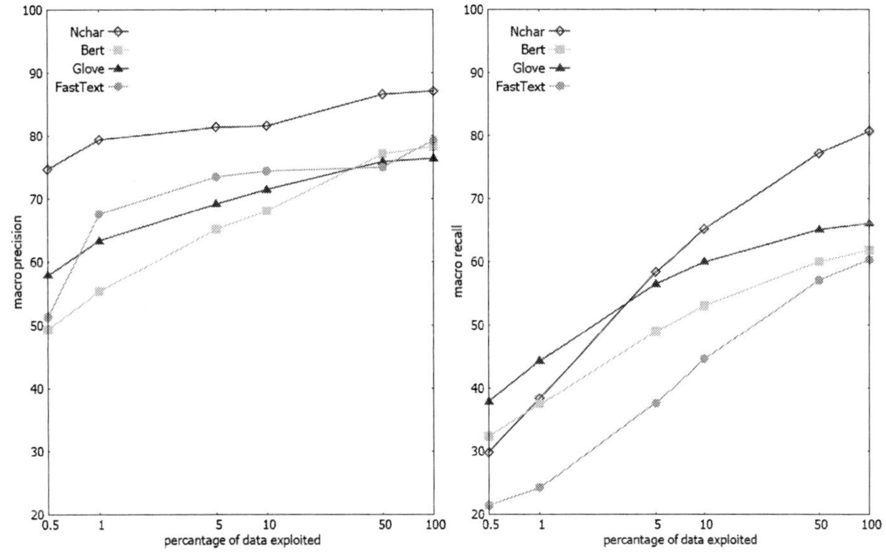

Figure 3: Macro Precision and Recall results for Event Subtype Classification on the different subsets of ACLED-C dataset.

or `Peaceful protest` event subtype versus `Protest with intervention`,

- vast majority of errors in general is due to wrongly classifying the event subtype as `Armed clash` (in the first row of the matrix one can observe clashes for 23 subtypes with the aforementioned event subtype), followed by errors resulting from misclassification of the subtype as `Attack`, which is most likely due to the fact that armed clashes and attacks constitute ca. 23% and 10% of all events resp., and

- finally, some more prominent observable clashes between event subtype misclassifications that go beyond the same main event and are worth mentioning are the ones that potentially result from similar vocabulary used (small nuances in the definition), e.g., the two following event descriptions were mis-classified by all approaches. [1] was supposed to be of type `Non-state actor overtakes territory` but has been classified as `Gov. regains terr.` Instead, [2] was supposed to be of type `Gov. regains terr` but has been classified as `Non-state actor overtakes territory.`

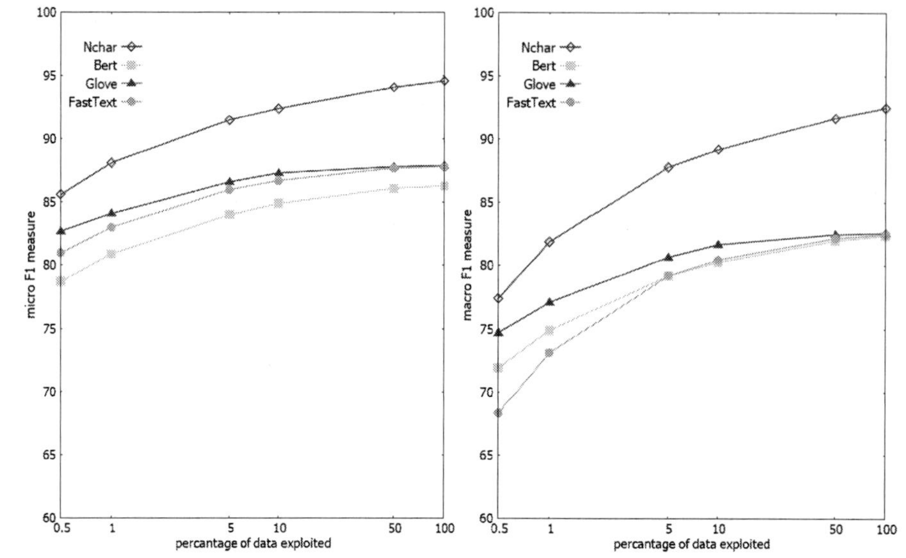

Figure 4: Micro and Macro F_1 measure results for Event Type Classification on the different subsets of ACLED-C dataset.

	Armed clash	Government regains territory	Non-state actor overtakes territory	Chemical weapon	Air/drone strike	Suicide bomb	Shelling/artillery/missile attack	Remote explosive/landmine/IED	Grenade	Sexual violence	Attack	Abduction/forced disappearance	Peaceful protest	Protest with intervention	Excessive force against protesters	Violent demonstration	Mob violence	Agreement	Arrests	Change to group/activity	Disrupted weapons use	Headquarters or base established	Looting/property destruction	Non-violent transfer of territory	Other
Armed clash	0.84	0.15	0.14	0.06	0.02	0.12	0.06	0.03	0.05	0.02	0.10	0.05	0	0	0.01	0.01	0.07	0.06	0.04	0.05	0.06	0.04	0.05	0.07	0.05
Government regains territory	0.02	0.63	0.13	0	0	0	0	0	0	0	0	0	0	0	0	0	0	0	0	0.01	0	0.03	0	0.10	0
Non-state actor overtakes territory	0.01	0.12	0.65	0	0	0	0	0	0	0	0	0	0	0	0	0	0	0	0	0	0	0	0	0.06	0.01
Chemical weapon	0	0	0	0.94	0	0	0	0	0	0	0	0	0	0	0	0	0	0	0	0	0	0	0	0	0
Air/drone strike	0.01	0	0	0	0.95	0.01	0.01	0.01	0	0	0	0	0	0	0	0	0	0	0	0.01	0.01	0	0.01	0	0.01
Suicide bomb	0	0	0	0	0	0.82	0	0	0	0	0	0	0	0	0	0	0	0	0	0	0	0	0	0	0
Shelling/artillery/missile attack	0.02	0.01	0	0	0.01	0	0.92	0.01	0	0	0	0	0	0	0	0	0	0	0	0	0.01	0.01	0.01	0	0
Remote explosive/landmine/IED	0.01	0	0	0	0	0	0	0.90	0.03	0	0.01	0	0	0	0	0	0	0	0	0	0.06	0	0.01	0.01	0.03
Grenade	0	0	0	0	0	0	0	0	0.85	0	0	0	0	0	0	0	0	0	0	0	0.01	0	0	0	0
Sexual violence	0	0	0	0	0	0	0	0	0	0.88	0.01	0	0	0	0	0	0	0	0	0	0	0	0	0	0
Attack	0.05	0.01	0.02	0	0	0.01	0	0.01	0.02	0.05	0.76	0.10	0	0.02	0.08	0.02	0.10	0.02	0.06	0.02	0	0.02	0.10	0.02	0.05
Abduction/forced disappearance	0	0	0	0	0	0	0	0	0	0	0.02	0.78	0	0	0	0	0	0.01	0.05	0.01	0	0.01	0.01	0.01	0.02
Peaceful protest	0	0	0	0	0	0	0	0	0	0.02	0.01	0.01	0.92	0.13	0.05	0.08	0.02	0.01	0.02	0.03	0	0	0.02	0.02	0.04
Protest with intervention	0	0	0	0	0	0	0	0	0	0	0	0	0.03	0.67	0.13	0.05	0.01	0	0.03	0	0	0	0	0	0.01
Excessive force against protesters	0	0	0	0	0	0	0	0	0	0	0	0	0	0.04	0.59	0.02	0	0	0	0	0	0	0	0	0
Violent demonstration	0	0	0	0	0	0	0	0	0	0.01	0.01	0	0.03	0.11	0.13	0.73	0.10	0	0.01	0.01	0	0	0.03	0	0.02
Mob violence	0.01	0	0	0	0	0.01	0	0	0.01	0.03	0.04	0	0.01	0.01	0.01	0.08	0.69	0	0.01	0.01	0	0	0.04	0.01	0.01
Agreement	0	0	0	0	0	0	0	0	0	0	0	0.01	0	0	0	0	0	0.69	0	0.02	0	0.01	0	0.02	0.03
Arrests	0	0	0	0	0	0	0	0	0	0	0	0.01	0	0.02	0	0	0	0.01	0.70	0.01	0.01	0	0	0	0
Change to group/activity	0	0.01	0.01	0	0	0	0	0	0	0	0	0.01	0	0	0	0	0	0.09	0.02	0.75	0.01	0.06	0.01	0.06	0.06
Disrupted weapons use	0	0	0	0	0	0.03	0	0.02	0.01	0	0	0	0	0	0	0	0	0	0.02	0.01	0.79	0	0.01	0	0.01
Headquarters or base established	0	0	0	0	0	0	0	0	0	0	0	0	0	0	0	0	0	0	0	0.02	0	0.77	0	0.02	0.01
Looting/property destruction	0	0	0	0	0	0	0	0	0.01	0	0.01	0.01	0	0	0	0	0.01	0.01	0	0.01	0.02	0	0.70	0.01	0.02
Non-violent transfer of territory	0	0.05	0.04	0	0	0	0	0	0	0	0	0	0	0	0	0	0	0.02	0	0.02	0	0.06	0	0.60	0.01
Other	0	0	0	0	0	0	0	0.01	0.01	0	0	0.01	0	0	0	0	0	0.06	0.01	0.03	0	0	0.01	0.02	0.61

Figure 5: The confusion matrix for Event Subtype classification using GLOVE word embeddings.

[1] on 25 january the ajdabiya shura council claimed to have retaken the 18 gate from the lna 21 border guards the gate southeast of the city was secured by the lna on 10 jan.

[2] rebels attacked the town of tin hama being held by gatia progovernment troops and briefly took over before the malian military intervened and chased the rebels out.

5. Conclusions

In this paper we reported on some preliminary experiments comparing various linguistically-lightweight approaches for fine-grained event classification based on short text snippets reporting on events. The results of our tests on a relatively large event corpus revealed that a TF-IDF-weighted character n-gram SVM-based model outperforms (reaching 83.5% macro and 92.4% micro F_1 score) SVM models that exploit various of-the-shelf pre-trained word embeddings as features.

While the results reported in this paper are promising and the event description in the ACLED corpus used for the evaluation strongly resemble the headlines and leading sentences of news articles reporting on events, one can only hypothesize that similar results could be obtained on real news data. Also, there are other more complex ways of exploiting word embeddings using neural architectures that were not explored in this work. Therefore, in order to get a more in-depth insight and more complete picture we intend to explore the performance of other shallow learners, including non-linear SVM models, decision trees and deployment of other type of word embedding-based approaches too, e.g. Sentence-BERT embeddings (Reimers and Gurevych, 2019) and tuning thereof for the particular task at hand. Furthermore, future work might also encompass: (a) exploring ways to combine the TF-IDF character n-gram and word embedding-based approaches to boost the performance, and (b) studying the impact of the length of the event descriptions on the overall performance.

Furthermore, we intend to create two additional corpora: (a) one consisting of real news article snippets reporting on events in order to study whether one can obtain similar performance to the one reported in this paper, and (b) a multilingual version of the ACLED corpus in order to study the portability of the approaches across languages, benefiting in particular from the existence of pre-trained multilingual word embeddings, such as the ones we experimented with in this paper.

The ACLED-C dataset and the corresponding word embedding vectors that were computed and used for carrying out the experiments reported in this paper are accessible at `https://jeodpp.jrc.ec.europa.eu/ftp/jrc-opendata/LANGUAGE-TECHNOLOGY/2020_annotated_event_dataset/ACLED-G_dataset/`. The The ACLED-C dataset is also available as one file[10] from `http://piskorski.waw.pl/resources/acled/ALL.zip`

6. Bibliographical References

ACLED. (2019). Armed Conflict Location & Event Data Project (ACLED) Codebook. Technical report. Accessed at: `https://www.acleddata.com/resources/general-guides/`.

Atkinson, M., Piskorski, J., Yangarber, R., and van der Goot, E. (2011). Multilingual Real-Time Event Extraction for Border Security Intelligence Gathering. In Uffe Kock Wiil, editor, *Open Source Intelligence and Counter-terrorism*. Springer, LNCS, Vol. 2.

Atkinson, M., Piskorski, J., Tanev, H., and Zavarella, V. (2017). On the Creation of a Security-Related Event Corpus. In *Proceedings of the Events and Stories in the News Workshop 2017*, pages 59–65, Vancouver, Canada. Association for Computational Linguistics.

Bengio, Y., Ducharme, R., Vincent, P., and Janvin, C. (2003). A neural probabilistic language model. *J. Mach. Learn. Res.*, 3:1137–1155.

Chesney, S., Jacquet, G., Steinberger, R., and Piskorski, J. (2017). Multi-word entity classification in a highly multilingual environment. *Proceedings of EACL 2017 Multi-Word Expressions Workshop*.

Chinchor, N. A. (1998). Overview of MUC-7. In *Seventh Message Understanding Conference (MUC-7): Proceedings of a Conference Held in Fairfax, Virginia, April 29 - May 1, 1998*.

Devlin, J., Chang, M.-W., Lee, K., and Toutanova, K. (2019). BERT: Pre-training of deep bidirectional transformers for language understanding. In *Proceedings of the 2019 Conference of the North American Chapter of the Association for Computational Linguistics: Human Language Technologies, Volume 1 (Long and Short Papers)*, pages 4171–4186, Minneapolis, Minnesota, June. Association for Computational Linguistics.

Doddington, G., Mitchell, A., Przybocki, M., Ramshaw, L., Strassel, S., and Weischedel, R. (2004). The automatic content extraction (ACE) program – tasks, data, and evaluation. In *Proceedings of the Fourth International Conference on Language Resources and Evaluation (LREC'04)*, Lisbon, Portugal, May. European Language Resources Association (ELRA).

Grave, E., Bojanowski, P., Gupta, P., Joulin, A., and Mikolov, T. (2018). Learning word vectors for 157 languages. In *Proceedings of the International Conference on Language Resources and Evaluation (LREC 2018)*.

Hong, Y., Zhang, J., Ma, B., Yao, J., Zhou, G., and Zhu, Q. (2011). Using cross-entity inference to improve event extraction. In *Proceedings of the 49th Annual Meeting of the Association for Computational Linguistics: Human Language Technologies*, pages 1127–1136, Portland, Oregon, USA, June. Association for Computational Linguistics.

Hürriyetoğlu, A., Yörük, E., Yüret, D., Yoltar, Ç., Gürel, B., Duruşan, F., and Mutlu, O. (2019). A task set proposal for automatic protest information collection across multiple countries. In Leif Azzopardi, et al., editors, *Advances in Information Retrieval*, pages 316–323, Cham. Springer International Publishing.

Joachims, T. (1998). Text categorization with support vector machines: Learning with many relevant features. In *European conference on machine learning*, pages 137–142. Springer.

King, G. and Lowe, W. (2003). An Automated Information Extraction Tool For International Conflict Data with Performance as Good as Human Coders. *International Organization*, 57:617–642.

LDC. (2008). Annotation Tasks and Specification.

[10] Each line contains the event description followed by (tab-separated) event type and subtype.

ONLINE: https://www.ldc.upenn.edu/collaborations/past-projects/ace/annotation-tasks-and-specifications.

Leetaru, K. and Schrodt, P. A. (2013). Gdelt: Global data on events, location, and tone, 1979–2012. In *ISA Annual Convention*, volume 2. Citeseer.

Liao, S. and Grishman, R. (2010). Using document level cross-event inference to improve event extraction. In *Proceedings of the 48th Annual Meeting of the Association for Computational Linguistics*, pages 789–797, Uppsala, Sweden, July. Association for Computational Linguistics.

Mikolov, T., Grave, E., Bojanowski, P., Puhrsch, C., and Joulin, A. (2018). Advances in pre-training distributed word representations. In *Proceedings of the International Conference on Language Resources and Evaluation (LREC 2018)*.

Nguyen, T. H. and Grishman, R. (2015). Event detection and domain adaptation with convolutional neural networks. In *Proceedings of the 53rd Annual Meeting of the Association for Computational Linguistics and the 7th International Joint Conference on Natural Language Processing (Volume 2: Short Papers)*, pages 365–371, Beijing, China, July. Association for Computational Linguistics.

Nguyen, T. H., Fauceglia, N., Rodriguez Muro, M., Hassanzadeh, O., Massimiliano Gliozzo, A., and Sadoghi, M. (2016). Joint learning of local and global features for entity linking via neural networks. In *Proceedings of COLING 2016, the 26th International Conference on Computational Linguistics: Technical Papers*, pages 2310–2320, Osaka, Japan, December. The COLING 2016 Organizing Committee.

Nugent, T., Petroni, F., Raman, N., Carstens, L., and Leidner, J. L. (2017). A comparison of classification models for natural disaster and critical event detection from news. In *2017 IEEE International Conference on Big Data, BigData 2017, Boston, MA, USA, December 11-14, 2017*, pages 3750–3759.

Ollagnier, A. and Williams, H. (2019). Classification and event identification using word embedding. In *Proceedings of CLEF*.

Pastor-Galindo, J., Nespoli, P., Gómez Mármol, F., and Martínez Pérez, G. (2020). The not yet exploited goldmine of osint: Opportunities, open challenges and future trends. *IEEE Access*, 8:10282–10304.

Pedregosa, F., Varoquaux, G., Gramfort, A., Michel, V., Thirion, B., Grisel, O., Blondel, M., Prettenhofer, P., Weiss, R., Dubourg, V., Vanderplas, J., Passos, A., David, Cournapeau, Brucher, M., Perrot, M., and Édouard Duchesnay. (2011). Scikit-learn: Machine learning in Python. *Journal of Machine Learning Research*, 12:2825–2830.

Pennington, J., Socher, R., and Manning, C. D. (2014). Glove: Global vectors for word representation. In *Empirical Methods in Natural Language Processing (EMNLP)*, pages 1532–1543.

Piskorski, J., Tanev, H., Atkinson, M., van der Goot, E., and Zavarella, V. (2011). In Ngoc Thanh Nguyen, editor, *Transactions on Computational Collective Intelligence*, pages 182–212. Springer Berlin Heidelberg, Berlin, Heidelberg.

Qin, Y.-P. and Wang, X.-K. (2009). Study on multi-label text classification based on svm. In *Fuzzy Systems and Knowledge Discovery, 2009. FSKD'09. Sixth International Conference on*, volume 1, pages 300–304. IEEE.

Raleigh, C., Linke, A., Hegre, H., and Karlsen, J. (2010). Introducing acled: An armed conflict location and event dataset: Special data feature. *Journal of Peace Research*, 47(5):651–660.

Reimers, N. and Gurevych, I. (2019). Sentence-BERT: Sentence embeddings using Siamese BERT-networks. In *Proceedings of the 2019 Conference on Empirical Methods in Natural Language Processing and the 9th International Joint Conference on Natural Language Processing (EMNLP-IJCNLP)*, pages 3982–3992, Hong Kong, China, November. Association for Computational Linguistics.

Sundheim, B. M. (1991). Overview of the third Message Understanding Evaluation and Conference. In *Third Message Uunderstanding Conference (MUC-3): Proceedings of a Conference Held in San Diego, California, May 21-23, 1991*.

Vaswani, A., Shazeer, N., Parmar, N., Uszkoreit, J., Jones, L., Gomez, A. N., Kaiser, u., and Polosukhin, I. (2017). Attention is all you need. In *Proceedings of the 31st International Conference on Neural Information Processing Systems*, NIPS'17, page 6000–6010, Red Hook, NY, USA. Curran Associates Inc.

Ward, M. D., Beger, A., Cutler, J., Dickenson, M., Dorff, C., and Radford, B. (2013). Comparing GDELT and ICEWS event data. *Analysis*, 21:267–297.

Yang, Y. and Liu, X. (1999). A re-examination of text categorization methods. In *Proceedings of the 22nd annual international ACM SIGIR conference on Research and development in information retrieval*, pages 42–49. ACM.

Yangarber, R., Etter, P. V., and Steinberger, R. (2008). Content Collection and Analysis in the Domain of Epidemiology. In *Proceedings of DrMED 2008: International Workshop on Describing Medical Web Resources at MIE 2008: the 21st International Congress of the European Federation for Medical Informatics 2008*, Goeteborg, Sweden.

Ye, Q., Zhang, Z., and Law, R. (2009). Sentiment classification of online reviews to travel destinations by supervised machine learning approaches. *Expert Systems with Applications*, 36(3):6527–6535.

Proceedings of AESPEN 2020, pages 35–41
Language Resources and Evaluation Conference (LREC 2020), Marseille, 11–16 May 2020

Seeing the Forest and the Trees: Detection and Cross-Document Coreference Resolution of Militarized Interstate Disputes

Benjamin J. Radford
University of North Carolina at Charlotte
benjamin.radford@uncc.edu

Abstract

Previous efforts to automate the detection of social and political events in text have primarily focused on identifying events described within single sentences or documents. Within a corpus of documents, these automated systems are unable to link event references—recognize singular events across multiple sentences or documents. A separate literature in computational linguistics on event coreference resolution attempts to link known events to one another within (and across) documents. I provide a data set for evaluating methods to identify certain political events in text and to link related texts to one another based on shared events. The data set, *Headlines of War*, is built on the *Militarized Interstate Disputes* data set and offers headlines classified by dispute status and headline pairs labeled with coreference indicators. Additionally, I introduce a model capable of accomplishing both tasks. The multi-task convolutional neural network is shown to be capable of recognizing events and event coreferences given the headlines' texts and publication dates.

Keywords: event data, event coreference resolution, event linking, political conflict

1. Introduction

The automation of political event detection in text has been of interest to political scientists for over two decades. Schrodt (1998) introduced KEDS, the Kansas Event Data System in the 1990s, an early piece of event coding software. Successors to KEDS include TABARI, JABARI-NLP, and now PETRARCH in its various incarnations (Schrodt, 2009; Schrodt et al., 2014). However, these tools rely primarily on performing pattern-matching within texts against dictionaries, limiting their ability to recognize singular events across multiple sentences or documents. This leads to unwanted duplication within event data sets and limits the types of detected events to those that are concisely summarized in a single line.

Social scientists have recently begun exploring machine learning-based approaches to coding particular types of political events (Beieler, 2016; Hürriyetoğlu et al., 2019; Radford, 2019). However, these efforts still mainly focus on classifying events at the sentence or document level. In this paper, I propose an approach to event-coding that is able to detect singular events at both the document (headline) level as well as across documents. Therefore, this challenge is not only a classification task but also a coreference prediction task; headlines are classified as pertaining to events and multiple headlines referring to the same event are identified as coreferencing the event.

This two-part challenge mirrors real-world cross-document event coreference detection. The first task is the identification of relevant events among a corpus that contains relevant (positive) and irrelevant (negative) events. The second task is to identify event coreferences across documents. Multiple articles may refer to the same event, and there may be an arbitrary number of distinct events within the corpus. This second task is conceptualized as link prediction wherein a link between articles signifies that they refer to the same event.

The data set described in this paper is available on Harvard Dataverse: https://doi.org/10.7910/DVN/8TEG5R.

Event linking, or coreference resolution, has been studied in the context of computer science and computational linguistics. This research is often framed within the larger problem of automated knowledge base population from text. Lu and Ng (2018) provide a review of research in this area over the previous two decades including discussion of standard data sets, evaluation methods, common linguistic features used for coreference resolution, and coreference resolution models. Notable datasets for coreference resolution include one built by Hong et al. (2016) using the Automated Content Extraction (ACE2005[1]) corpus, a data set produced by Song et al. (2018) in support of the Text Analysis Conference Knowledge Base Population effort, and the EventCorefBank (ECB) and ECB+[2] data sets (Bejan and Harabagiu, 2010; Cybulska and Vossen, 2014).

Advances in event linking also promise to enhance automated event data generation for social science applications. Event data sets like ICEWS, GDELT, and Pheonix suffer from duplicate event records when single events are reported multiple times by multiple sources (Boschee et al., 2015; Leetaru and Schrodt, 2013; Althaus et al., 2019). Typically, duplicated records are removed via heuristics based on the uniqueness of event attribute sets. Event linking techniques may allow event data sets like to these to better represent complex phenomena (e.g., wars) that are described across multiple documents while avoiding the duplication problem.

The paper proceeds as follows. I first describe a novel data set designed to evaluate performance on cross-document event detection. I then introduce a model capable of both event detection and cross-document coreference prediction and evaluate its performance on out-of-sample data. The paper concludes with a discussion of the limitations of the evaluation data set and suggested directions for future research.

[1] http://projects.ldc.upenn.edu/ace
[2] http://www.newsreader-project.eu/results/data/the-ecb-corpus/

2. Data

I introduce here a task-specific evaluation data set referred to as the *Headlines of War* (HoW) data set. HoW takes the form of a node list that describes news story headlines and an edge list that represents coreference links between headlines. HoW draws headline and coreference data from two sources. The first is the *Militarized Interstate Disputes* data set (MIDS) version 3. MIDS provides a set of newspaper headlines that coreference interstate disputes. *The New York Times* (NYT) provides a second source of headlines that constitute the negative (non-coreferential) samples.

2.1. MIDS

MIDS is a standard in political science and international relations.[3] It is published by the Correlates of War Project, an effort that dates to 1963 (Singer and Small, 1966). A MID is a collection of "incidents involving the deliberate, overt, government-sanctioned, and government-directed threat, display, or use of force between two or more states" (Maoz et al., 2019). As such, many MIDs, and the incidents they comprise, are macro-level events that may occur over an extended period of time and comprise many smaller events. For example, a number of ceasefire violations in Croatia in February, 1992, together constitute incident 3555003. 3555003 is one of many incidents that make up MID 3555, the Croatian War for Independence. MIDs and the incidents they comprise tend to be larger-scale than the events found in typical event data sets.

MIDS differs from automated event data in several ways. Automated event data sets (referred to herein simply as "event data") like GDELT, ICEWS, and Phoenix typically document discrete events that are easily described in a single sentence. This is due, in part, to the fact that the necessary coding software parses stories sentence-by-sentence and uses pattern-matching to identify the key components of an event within a given sentence. This leads to data sets that feature simple events and often include duplicate records of events. Failure to deduplicate led, in one case, to an incident in which a popular blog was forced to issue corrections due to the over-counting of kidnapping events in GDELT (Chalabi, 2014).

Because it is coded manually, MIDS features more complex events than automated event data systems are capable of producing. MIDs comprise incidents, and incidents may (or may not) themselves comprise a number of actions that would each constitute their own entry in an automated event data set. Because each MID is coded from a number of news sources, duplication of disputes is not a concern; human coders are capable of mapping stories from multiple news sources to the single incident or dispute to which they all refer.

MIDS provides HoW with positive class labels (i.e.,, headlines associated with MIDs) and positive coreferences (pairs of headlines associated with common MIDs). I use the third version of MIDS due to the availability of a subset of the source headlines used to produce the data set (Ghosn et al., 2004).[4]

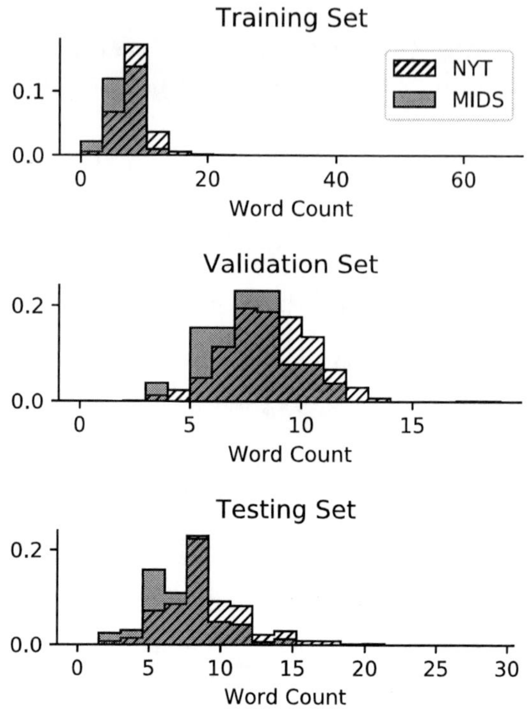

Figure 1: Sentence length in words by HoW subset.

2.2. The New York Times

Negative samples, headlines not associated with militarized interstate disputes, are drawn from *The New York Times* for the same period as that covered by MIDs 3.0: 1992–2001.[5] NYT headlines and their associated sections (e.g., World, US, Sports, ...) are available from https://spiderbites.nytimes.com. HoW contains only samples from the World section. This is to ensure that the resulting task is sufficiently difficult. Articles drawn from the World section are more likely to mirror the MIDs headlines in tone and substance; distinguishing between MIDS headlines and NYT World headlines should, therefore, be more difficult than it would be if articles from all sections were sampled.

2.3. Putting it Together: HoW

The HoW data are partitioned into three parts: training, validation, and testing. Partitioning is performed by year to make it unlikely that a single MID incident's reference headlines are found across all three partitions. An unfortunate consequence of doing so is that it is difficult to control

[3]The *Militarized Interstate Disputes* data set will be referred to as MIDS while an individual dispute will be referred to as MID (plural: MIDs). A MID incident will sometimes be referred to as MIDI.

[4]The source data are available at https://correlatesofwar.org/data-sets/MIDs. An effort to update HoW with MIDS version 4 headlines is underway.

[5]MIDs 3.0 only includes those conflicts from 1992 that were ongoing in 1993. For simplicity, NYT headlines are sampled from January 1, 1992.

	Training	Validation	Testing
Start date (01/01)	1992	1997	1998
End date (12/31)	1996	1997	2001
Headlines	4,987	966	13,515
MID headlines	123	26	108
¬MID headlines	4,864	940	13,407
Characters	249,092	47,018	756,230
Unique MIDs	10	6	3
Unique Incidents	26	6	4
Links	3,378	678	30,342
Positive links	563	113	5,057
Negative links	2,815	565	25,285

Table 1: Summary statistics of HoW data set partitions.

the relative sizes of each partition. MID incidents are not evenly distributed across years, and so the validation set is smaller (in terms of headline-pairs) than the training set, which is, in turn, smaller than the testing set.

Summary statistics for each partition of HoW are given in Table 1. Not all MIDs and MID incidents during the relevant time periods are included. This is due to the fact that the MIDS source data do not report headlines for all incidents. In many cases, page numbers and sections numbers are provided in lieu of the headline text itself. Therefore, HoW contains a total of only 18 unique MIDs (with one appearing in two partitions) and 36 unique incidents.

Each partition comprises a node list and an edge list. The node list contains the headline text, publication date, associated MID identifier and incident identifier (if applicable), and an indicator of whether the headline is a positive (MID) sample or a negative (NYT World) sample. The edge list includes positive links between headlines if they refer to the same MID incident along with a sample of negative links drawn randomly from NYT World and MIDS headlines. Therefore, a single MID incident is represented in the edge list by a fully-connected subgraph of headlines.

Figure 1 depicts the distribution of headline lengths, in words, for each of the HoW subsets. The average headline length is just under nine words.

3. Modeling Strategy

To demonstrate that HoW presents a tractable pair of tasks, I describe a model capable of accomplishing, to a degree, both headline classification and link prediction on the data set. The model is a multi-task neural network that takes as input numerical representations of two headlines and the reciprocal of $1 + (\Delta publicationdates)$. The model then predicts the MID status of both headlines, $headline_a$ and $headline_b$, and whether or not the headlines refer to the same MID incident.

3.1. Preparing the Headlines

The first step of modeling is to remove all punctuation from the headlines' texts. For convenience, headlines are zero-padded such that they are all of equal length. Headlines are then tokenized and word vectors are substituted for each

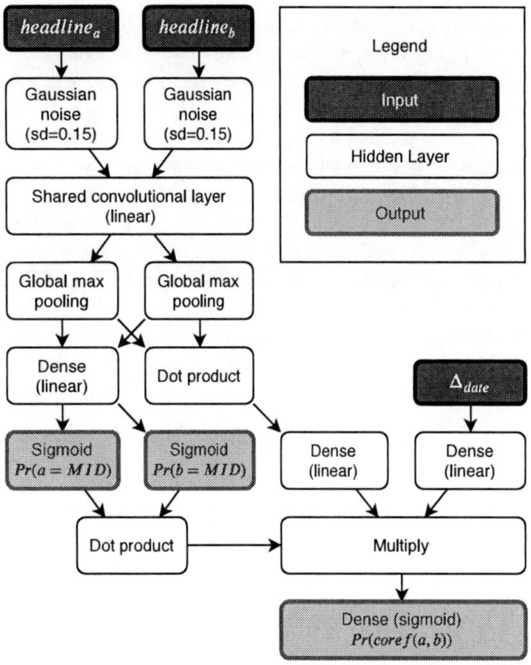

Figure 2: Model architecture for headline classification and corefence prediction.

word.[6] Pre-trained word vectors are obtained from Facebook's fastText (Mikolov et al., 2018). FastText is selected because it is able to produce word vectors for out-of-sample words—those that it has not previously seen. Word vectors are length 300 real-valued vectors that represent words in such a way that semantically and syntactically related words share similar vectors.

3.2. Model Architecture

The model itself comprises a single convolutional layer of size $300 \times 15 \times 3$ and three dense, fully-connected layers for predicting MID status and coreference status. For a given input pair, the model outputs three predictions:

$$Pr\,(a = MID|headline_a)$$
$$Pr\,(b = MID|headline_b)$$
$$Pr\,(coref(a,b)|headline_a, headline_b, \Delta_{date})$$

where $coref(a,b)$ indicates that $headline_a$ and $headline_b$ refer to the same MID incident and $\Delta_{date} = 1/(1 + |date_a - date_b|)$. The overall model architecture is depicted in Figure 2. The model contains 13,537 trainable parameters, 13,515 of which are in the convolutional layer.

The intuition behind the model is as follows. MID classification should be the same task regardless of whether the input headline is a or b. Therefore, the convolutional layer and subsequent densely-connected layer are shared between the two. Combined, this outputs a predicted probability that a given headline describes a MID incident. Af-

[6]When a word vector cannot be obtained for a given token, that token is simply dropped.

ter the convolutional layer and an element-wise maximum value pooling layer, the dot product of the hidden states representing $headline_a$ and $headline_b$ is computed; this represents the similarity of the two headlines. This value is multiplied by the predicted probabilities that each headline represents a MID incident as well as by a linear function of the time difference (in days) between the two headlines. A sigmoid activation is applied to this product; this value represents the probability of a MID incident coreference between $headline_a$ and $headline_b$. Therefore, MID incident coreferences are most likely when the model predicts that both $headline_a$ and $headline_b$ describe MID incidents, when the hidden state representations of those headlines are most similar, and when the publication date difference between the headlines is small.

3.3. Training Procedure

The model is trained for 100 epochs on batches of 64 training samples. The validation set is used for parameter tuning. The testing set remains unobserved until the final model is selected. Because the model must predict three binary responses, the loss function is the unweighted sum of the three binary cross-entropy terms given in Equation 1. The model is fit using Nadam, a variant of the Adam optimizer with Nesterov momentum (Dozat, 2016).

$$\begin{aligned} Loss = &- \textstyle\sum_{i=0}^{1} y_i^{headline_a} \log\left(Pr(a=i)\right) \\ &- \textstyle\sum_{j=0}^{1} y_j^{headline_b} \log\left(Pr(b=j)\right) \\ &- \textstyle\sum_{k=0}^{1} y_k^{coref(a,b)} \log\left(Pr(coref(a,b)=k)\right) \end{aligned} \quad (1)$$

This model is similar in some aspects to the one introduced by Krause et al. (2016). Major differences include the use of fastText vectors here rather than word2vec vectors, the requirement in this model that it not only identifies coreferential headlines but also that it discriminates between events and non-events, and the lack of additional contextual information about event pairs.[7]

3.4. Task Evaluation

Tasks 1 and 2 are both conceptualized as binary classification and therefore a number of evaluation metrics are available. Here, I report classification accuracy[8], precision[9], recall[10], F_1-score[11], and the area under the receiver operating characteristic curve (AUC) for both tasks. Due to class imbalance, I also report BLANC scores to better capture model performance among event links and non-links (Recasens and Hovy, 2011). The equivalent statistics, referred to as macro averaged precision, recall, and F_1-score, are reported for MID classification.

In out-of-sample evaluation (i.e., validation and test set performance) I use no information about the headline classes (MID incident versus non-incident) or coreferences. In other words, link predictions are conditioned on the texts and publication dates of headlines only and not on the MID status of a given headline.

[7] Krause et al. (2016) include type compatibility, position in discourse, realis match, and argument overlap.

[8] % classified correctly

[9] $\frac{T_p}{T_p+F_p}$

[10] $\frac{T_p}{T_p+F_n}$

[11] $F_1 = \left(2 \cdot \frac{precision \cdot recall}{precision+recall}\right)$

	Pre.	Rec.	F_1	Acc.	AUC
a. MIDI classification (positive class)					
Training set	0.73	0.47	0.57	0.97	0.73
Validation set	0.89	0.23	0.36	0.85	0.61
Testing set	0.27	0.19	0.22	0.99	0.59
b. MIDI classification (macro average)					
Training set	0.85	0.73	0.78		
Validation set	0.87	0.61	0.64		
Testing set	0.63	0.59	0.61		
c. Coref prediction (positive class)					
Training set	1.00	0.90	0.95	0.98	1.00
Validation set	1.00	0.76	0.86	0.96	1.00
Testing set	0.99	0.45	0.62	0.91	1.00
d. Coref prediction (BLANC)					
Training set	0.99	0.95	0.97		
Validation set	0.98	0.88	0.92		
Testing set	0.95	0.72	0.78		

Table 2: Performance statistics across partitions of HoW. Positive class (*a* and *c*) denotes an occurrence of a MID incident or a MID incident coreference, respectively. Macro average and BLANC (*b* and *d*) indicate that the reported statistics have been averaged across classes with each class having been assigned equal weight.

MID	Pr	Headline
False	0.91	Serbs Advance in Kosovo, Imperiling...
True	0.90	Feuding factions meet in Congo...
True	0.87	Significant Rwandan troop movement ...
False	0.87	Serbs Stone Albanians in Divided Ko...
True	0.86	Zimbabwean troops deployed in Congo...
False	0.85	Attack in Baghdad...
False	0.83	Clashes in Zimbabwe...
True	0.82	Zimbabwe wins major battle in Congo...
True	0.80	Kabila moving against rebellious tr...
False	0.80	U.S. Cutbacks in Yemen...

Table 3: Top ten headlines with respect to predicted probability of describing a MID.

4. Results

I turn now to an assessment of the model's performance on both tasks: MID classification at the headline level and coreference prediction between pairs of headlines. In this analysis, only $headline_a$ results are included when assessing MID classification. This is to prevent unintentional repeat counting of headlines that appear as both $headline_a$ and $headline_b$ in different training example pairs.

The model achieves high precision for coreference predic-

ID	Headline
A	Sudanese plane bombed Ugandan town aid ...
B	uganda condemns sudanese air attack...
C	One Dies as Navy Jets Collide Off Turkey...
D	U.S. to Change Strategy in Narcotics Fig...
E	Heading for an African War...
F	DRC gun running a rumour...
G	Rwanda needs and will get a buffer zone...
H	Farmers Protest Against Fox in Mexico Ci...
I	South Koreans Challenge Northerner on U....

Table 4: Selected headlines from Figure 3

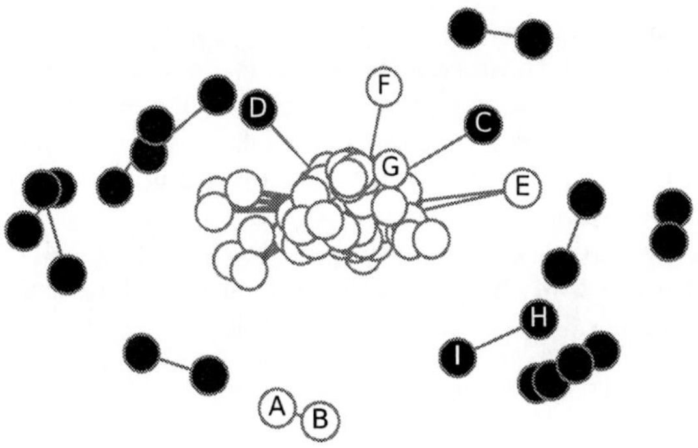

Figure 3: Predicted coreferences (edges) between headlines (nodes). White nodes are true MIDS headlines; black nodes are NYT World headlines. The central cluster primarily corresponds to MID incident 4339. The *A-B* pair corresponds to MID incident 4248003.

tion but lower precision for MID classification: 0.99 and 0.27 on the testing set, respectively. Relatively high false negative rates mean that recall is low for both tasks: 0.19 for MIDI classification and 0.45 for coreference prediction. However, considering the class imbalance present for both tasks and apparent in Table 1, the macro averaged or BLANC adjusted statistics are also reported. This is recommended in previous work on coreference resolution (Krause et al., 2016). The model fares better for both tasks when taking this imbalance into account and achieves recall values of 0.59 and 0.72 for classification and coreference prediction, respectively. Table 2 provides a full set of results for all three partitions. The final column of Table 2 reports the area under the receiver operating characteristic curve (AUC). AUC can be interpreted as the probability that a randomly selected positive example will be assigned higher predicted probability of belonging to the positive class than will a randomly selected negative example. The very high accuracy and AUC scores (near 1.0) can be attributed to the high recall of the classifiers with respect to the majority negative class. The table reveals overfitting to the training set on which the model consistently achieves its highest scores.

Because content relevant to militarized interstate disputes often appears in the NYT World section, the HoW data set currently contains a significant number of false negative headlines. Table 3 reproduces the top 10 highest scoring headlines with respect to their predicted probabilities of describing a MID. Some of the reported non-MID headlines clearly refer to MIDs.[12]

Figure 3 depicts predicted coreferences in the test set. Two of four MID incidents are present. A selection of headlines labeled in Figure 3 is provided in Table 4. The four MID incidents present in the HoW test set are 4248001, 4248003, 4283012, 4339, of which coreferences are identified among two or more headlines referring to 4339 and 4248003. 4339 is the Congo War. 4248001 and 4248003 are incidents between Uganda and Sudan during 1998. 4283012 is an incident between the UK and Afghanistan during the 2001 invasion of Afghanistan.

5. Discussion

The HoW data set comes with a number of caveats discussed below. The negative sampling is performed by first subsetting MIDS 3.0 into the training, testing, and validation sets. Then, negative samples are picked at a rate of $5\times$ for every positive MID story pair (i.e., edge). This scale factor is selected arbitrarily and results in a sparse graph.[13] Many negative samples describe MIDs themselves and should not be labeled as negative. No negative samples have been manually corrected and at least some false negatives can be expected. Negative samples are drawn only from the NYT World section while the MIDS 3.0 headlines are drawn from many diverse (English language) sources. Unfortunately, a representative corpus of headlines for negative sampling was unavailable at the time of writing.

Not all sources in MIDS are documented with enough specificity to identify the relevant headline. Some MID incidents only reference a section or page number and not a headline. A future step in the development of HoW will seek to identify the original source data for MID incidents that currently lack headline text to improve the coverage of MIDs over the period in question. Longer-term, additional data sources may provide event types beyond MIDs and therefore allow researchers to evaluate the out-of-class generalizability of cross-document event detection methods. In the near term, the more comprehensive headline data set for MIDS 4 (2002–2010) is being used to extend HoW and address the high proportion of missing MID incidents in HoW.

The decision made here was to partition HoW by date. This has the advantage of offering a simple explanation of how the partitions differ from one another: they cover distinct date ranges. It also allows researchers to consider the impact of the temporal proximity of two headlines on their likelihood of being associated with the same event. In that way, date-based partitioning imitates the likely real-world

[12]Because these non-MID headlines are from NYT, they are not associated with a MID in HoW. I hope to reduce false negatives in future iterations of HoW.

[13]While a negative sampling ratio of 5 to 1 is chosen arbitrarily, it does follow the standard in the literature for negative sampling skipgram models like word2vec (Mikolov et al., 2013).

scenario of cross-document event detection: near real-time monitoring. However, it also means that models fit to the training data set may generalize poorly to the testing data set since the testing data set represents events from up to five years later in time. Partitioning by time in such a way makes it difficult to control the number of positive-class observations per set. Down-sampling headlines from MIDS may help to manage partition balance but at the cost of even fewer positive MID headline examples.

6. Conclusion

HoW offers a novel evaluation data set for researchers interested in automated event data and coreference resolution. Conceptualizing event data generation as a two-task problem of detection and coreference resolution will allow future efforts to better identify complex social phenomena that may otherwise be invisible given existing sentence and document-level event coding strategies. It also has implications for deduplication: the ability to automatically detect event coreferences across documents may help to reduce the number of duplicate event records that result from coverage across multiple sources.

Future efforts should seek to build on HoW by including multiple classes of events or incidents.[14] Additionally, strategies for identifying true negative samples rather than relying on the assumption that all non-MIDS headlines are negative samples will help to more precisely evaluate model performance.

7. Bibliographical References

Althaus, S., Bajjalieh, J., Carter, J. F., Peyton, B., and Shalmon, D. A. (2019). *Cline Center Historical Phoenix Event Data*. Cline Center for Advanced Social Research., December.

Beieler, J. (2016). Generating politically-relevant event data. *Proceedings of 2016 EMNLP Workshop on Natural Language Processing and Computational Social Science*, pages 37–42.

Bejan, C. and Harabagiu, S. (2010). Unsupervised event coreference resolution with rich linguistic features. In *Proceedings of the 48th Annual Meeting of the Association for Computational Linguistics*, pages 1412–1422, Uppsala, Sweden, July. Association for Computational Linguistics.

Boschee, E., Lautenschlager, J., O'Brien, S., Shellman, S., Starz, J., and Ward, M. (2015). Bbn accent event coding evaluation.updated v01.pdf. In *ICEWS Coded Event Data*. Harvard Dataverse.

Chalabi, M. (2014). Mapping kidnappings in nigeria (updated). online, May. https://fivethirtyeight.com/features/mapping-kidnappings-in-nigeria/.

Cybulska, A. and Vossen, P. (2014). Using a sledgehammer to crack a nut? lexical diversity and event coreference resolution. In *Proceedings of the 9th international conference on Language Resources and Evaluation (LREC2014)*.

[14]The previously mentioned event coreference resolution data sets contain multiple event types.

Dozat, T. (2016). Incorporating nesterov momentum into adam. http://cs229.stanford.edu/proj2015/054_report.pdf.

Ghosn, F., Palmer, G., and Bremer, S. (2004). The mid3 data set, 1993–2001: Procedures, coding rules, and description. *Conflict Management and Peace Science*, 21:133–154.

Hong, Y., Zhang, T., O'Gorman, T., Horowit-Hendler, S., Ji, H., and Palmer, M. (2016). Building a cross-document event-event relation corpus. *Proceedings of LAW X - The 10th Linguistic Annotation Workshop*, pages 1–6.

Hürriyetoğlu, A., Yörük, E., Yüret, D., Çağrı Yoltar, Gürel, B., Duruşan, F., Mutlu, O., and Akdemir, A. (2019). Overview of clef 2019 lab protestnews: Extracting protests from news in a cross-context setting. In *Experimental IR Meets Multilinguality, Multimodality, and Interaction*, pages 425–432, Cham. Springer International Publishing.

Krause, S., Xu, F., Uszkoreit, H., and Weissenborn, D. (2016). Event linking with sentential features from convolutional neural networks. *Proceedings of the 20th SIGNLL Conference on Computational Natural Language Learning (CoNLL)*, pages 239–249.

Leetaru, K. and Schrodt, P. A. (2013). Gdelt: Global data on events, location, and tone. *ISA Annual Convention*.

Lu, J. and Ng, V. (2018). Event coreference resolution: A survey of two decades of research. In *Proceedings of the Twenty-Seventh International Joint Conference on Artificial Intelligence, IJCAI-18*, pages 5479–5486. International Joint Conferences on Artificial Intelligence Organization, 7.

Maoz, Z., Johnson, P. L., Kaplan, J., Ogunkoya, F., and Shreve, A. P. (2019). The dyadic militarized interstate disputes (mids) dataset version 3.0: Logic, characteristics, and comparisons to alternative datasets. *Journal of Conflict Resolution*, 63(3):811–835.

Mikolov, T., Sutskever, I., Chen, K., Corrado, G., and Dean, J. (2013). Distributed representations of words and phrases and their compositionality. In *Proceedings of the 26th International Conference on Neural Information Processing Systems - Volume 2*, NIPS'13, page 3111–3119, Red Hook, NY, USA. Curran Associates Inc.

Mikolov, T., Grave, E., Bojanowski, P., Puhrsch, C., and Joulin, A. (2018). Advances in pre-training distributed word representations. In *Proceedings of the International Conference on Language Resources and Evaluation (LREC 2018)*.

Radford, B. J. (2019). Automated dictionary generation for political eventcoding. *Political Science Research and Methods*, page 1–15.

Recasens, M. and Hovy, E. H. (2011). Blanc: Implementing the rand index for coreference evaluation. *Natural Langauge Engineering*, 17(4):485–510.

Schrodt, P. A., Beieler, J., and Idris, M. (2014). Three's a charm?: Open event data coding with el:diablo, petrarch, and the open event data alliance.

Schrodt, P. A. (1998). Keds: Kansas event data system.

version 1.0.

Schrodt, P. A. (2009). Tabari: Textual analysis by augmented replacement instructions, version 0.7.

Singer, D. J. and Small, M. (1966). Formal alliances, 1815-1939. *Journal of Peace Research*, 3:1–31.

Song, Z., Bies, A., Mott, J., Li, X., Strassel, S., and Caruso, C. (2018). Cross-document, cross-language event coreference annotation using event hoppers. In *Proceedings of the Eleventh International Conference on Language Resources and Evaluation (LREC 2018)*, Miyazaki, Japan, May. European Language Resources Association (ELRA).

Proceedings of AESPEN 2020, pages 42–48
Language Resources and Evaluation Conference (LREC 2020), Marseille, 11–16 May 2020

Conflict Event Modelling: Research Experiment and Event Data Limitations

Matina Halkia, Stefano Ferri, Michail Papazoglou, Marie-Sophie Van Damme, Dimitrios Thomakos
European Commission, Joint Research Centre (JRC), European Commission, Joint Research Centre (JRC), Unisystems S.A, Piksel Ltd, Unisystems S.A
Via E. Fermi 2749 Ispra Italy, Via E. Fermi 2749 Ispra Italy, Via Michelangelo Buonarroti 39 Milano Italy, Via Breda 176 Milano Italy, Rue Edward Steichen 26, Luxembourg
{Matina.HALKIA, Stefano.FERRI}@ec.europa.eu
{Michail.PAPAZOGLOU, Marie-Sophie.VAN-DAMME, Dimitrios.THOMAKOS}@ext.ec.europa.eu

Abstract

This paper presents the conflict event modelling experiment, conducted at the Joint Research Centre of the European Commission, particularly focusing on the limitations of the input data. This model is under evaluation as to potentially complement the Global Conflict Risk Index (GCRI), a conflict risk model supporting the design of European Union's conflict prevention strategies. The model aims at estimating the occurrence of material conflict events, under the assumption that an increase in material conflict events goes along with a decrease in material and verbal cooperation. It adopts a Long-Short Term Memory Cell Recurrent Neural Network on country-level actor-based event datasets that indicate potential triggers to violent conflict such as demonstrations, strikes, or elections-related violence. The observed data and the outcome of the model predictions consecutively, consolidate an early warning alarm system that signals abnormal social unrest upheavals, and appears promising as an approach towards a conflict trigger model. However, event-based systems still require overcoming certain obstacles related to the quality of the input data and the event classification method.

Keywords: Early Warning System, actor-based event datasets, conflict prevention

1. Introduction

Quantitative modelling studies aiming to predict future conflicts, consider the number of casualties as a proxy for conflict intensity, using datasets such as the Armed Conflict Location & Event Data (ACLED) and Uppsala Conflict Data Program/Peace Research Institute Oslo (UCDP/PRIO) (Hegre et al., 2013; Szayna et al., 2017; Halkia et al., 2020). While the correlation between conflict intensity and the number of battle casualties is plausible, it does not consider conflict development stages (Qiao et al., 2017), as well as the complexity of events like protests, demonstrations, election violence, or even tension relief events such as diplomatic cooperation.

The Peace and Stability team at the European Commission's Joint Research Centre has developed a conflict event modelling algorithm (Halkia et al., 2019), which unlike the original structural conflict risk model based on statistical regressions (Halkia et al., 2017b, a, 2020), integrates and disentangles every stage of the conflict development or de-escalation cycle.

In this paper, we discuss two available news media datasets tested for this experimental conflict event model and their limitations: (i) the Global Data on Events Location and Tone (GDELT) project and (ii) the Integrated Crisis Early Warning System (ICEWS) Dataverse dataset. Both are based on the Conflict and Mediation Event Observations Event and Actor Codebook (CAMEO) classification.

The CAMEO codebook classifies event data in four primary classes, called QuadClass, i.e. verbal cooperation (Q_1), material cooperation (Q_2), verbal conflict (Q_3), and material conflict (Q_4). These primary classes are subdivided into 20 major categories and several sections, so as to create a detailed classification scale (Schrodt, 2012), following the typical evolution stages of social unrest; appeal, accusation, refuse, escalation, and finally protests/riots (Qiao et al., 2017). Social unrest events, that initially start as a demonstration to the public or the government, often escalate into general chaos, resulting in violence, riots, sabotage, and other forms of crime and social disorder. The Deep Learning (DL) methodology adopted to model the actor-based conflict events is a Long-Short Term Memory (LSTM) Cell Recurrent Neural Network (RNN). Besides this DL model, we have set up an early warning alarm system to signal abnormal social unrest upheavals.

Although the experimental conflict event model, through the DL and early warning alarm, is able to predict the materialization of a conflict on a monthly basis, event-based systems require supplementary research to offset the databases' shortcomings, such as automated data validation, new classifiers and dictionaries.

Section 2 presents the various datasets and their limitations; Section 3 explains the model and methodology proposed for the experimental conflict event model, whereas Section 4 presents the results. Finally, Section 5 and 6 respectively discuss the model's feasibility and steps forward.

2. Event Datasets Using the Conflict and Mediation Event Observations Event and Actor Codebook (CAMEO) Classification

The Global Database of Events, Language, and Tone Project (GDELT) and the Integrated Crisis Early Warning

System (ICEWS) Dataverse (ICEWS) are arguably the largest currently available event data collections in social science, which gather broad amounts of news items from various sources around the world. During their brief existence, they have been among the most influential datasets in terms of their impact on academic research and policy advice. In order to fulfil the purposes of this paper, we investigate the use of these two news media datasets as possible inputs for the experimental conflict event model and discuss their limitations[1].

2.1 Global Database of Events, Language, and Tone (GDELT) Project

The GDELT project is an on-going attempt to monitor print, broadcast web news media in over 100 languages from all over the world, almost real-time (GDELT, 2019). It is worth emphasizing that the GDELT dataset is updated every 15 minutes, meaning that there is a continuous flow of records integrating the database.

So far, researchers rarely aim at utilizing GDELT to make predictions about social unrest and only a few scholars have conducted predictions using GDELT, as it has been criticised for abundant duplicate returns. Alikhani (2014) attempted to use GDELT with linear regression models, while Yonamine (2013) studied the dataset for time series forecasting. More recent papers use GDELT for frequent subgraphs mining (Qiao et al., 2017) or artificial intelligence applications (Smith et al., 2018).

To our knowledge, one study has used the GDELT data to measure conflict intensity (Levin, Ali & Crandall, 2018). In their article, however, Levin, Ali and Crandall consider the monthly time series of the absolute number of events occurring in the CAMEO Q_4 subclasses or take a MaxMin normalization over their time series (i.e. normalization between zero and one based on the minimum and maximum values in the time series of each country). This conflict event modelling approach presented here, additionally evaluates the increase in the proportion of the various QuadClasses over the total number of events. Although the absolute and normalized number of events under each CAMEO QuadClass are giving important information, the conflict cycle development is better captured in its entire complexity when considering the analysis in proportions.

The major shortcoming of the GDELT project is the fact that the monitoring is based on simple keywords, which may lead to a collection of irrelevant records (noise). Furthermore, the automated codebook algorithm is not publicly available, which does not allow investigation on the source of potential errors in the news classification. However, as the source URL is given, we can undertake sample validation tests in order to detect misclassified events.

2.2 Integrated Crisis Early Warning System (ICEWS) Dataverse

The ICEWS program is a comprehensive, integrated, automated, generalizable, and validated system to monitor, assess, and forecast national, sub-national, and internal crises (Lockheed Martin, 2019). ICEWS has been discussed in the conflict prediction research literature (Tikuisis, Carment & Samy, 2013; Ward et al., 2013; Yonamine, 2013) as well as in relation to the coding of political events (Schrodt & Van Brackle, 2013).

The ICEWS program is temporally restricted as it scans news on a daily basis only since October 2018 and on a monthly basis since 1995. No data is available before 1995. Another limitation is that validating event classification is cumbersome and does not facilitate identifying the source of the record for the analyst. Hence, the cost of the validation effort is disproportionate.

According to Ward et al. (2013), who compared the GDELT and ICEWS datasets, *"it is clear that both databases pick up major events remarkably well. The volume of GDELT data is very much larger than the corresponding ICEWS data [...] It seems clear, however, that GDELT over-states the number of events by a substantial margin, but ICEWS misses some events as well"*.

3. Methodology

3.1 Deep Learning Event based Modelling

Most of the social unrest events, that initially start as a public demonstration against the government, often escalate into general chaos, resulting in riots, sabotage, and other forms of crime and social disorder (Qiao et al., 2017). Predicting these events can therefore be formulated as a sequence classification problem that identifies any possible stage of events that potentially lead to social unrest.

The proposed event-based model built upon the CAMEO classification to predict social unrest assumes that an increase in material and verbal conflict events goes along with a decrease in material and verbal cooperation. CAMEO classifies significant occurrence of supportive statements, requests and engagements in diplomatic cooperation as Verbal Cooperation (Q_1), while collaborative investigations, engagements in material cooperation, and provision of aid as Material Cooperation

[1] There are more available datasets but we cannot overcome their present limitations i.e. limited time series (e.g. Phoenix_RT from Oct. 2017 to today, Cline Center Historical Phoenix Event Data (Phoenix) up to 2015), and limited sources (e.g. Cline Center Historical Phoenix Event Data).

(Q_2). On the other hand, disapprovals, objections, and complaints, threats, rejection of cooperation and civilian demonstrations are assigned to Verbal Conflict (Q_3). Finally, CAMEO names as Material Conflict (Q_4) all military or police moves, repression and violence against civilians, use of conventional and unconventional forms of violence as well as mass violence (Schrodt, 2012).

When observing an increasing trend of news articles reported as Verbal Conflict (Q_3) and/or Material Conflict (Q_4) with respect to the total number of articles, the model is able to measure an increase in conflict related tensions.

The historical time series of Verbal Cooperation (Q_1), Material Cooperation (Q_2), Verbal Conflict (Q_3), and Material Conflict (Q_4) quantify and allow us to grasp the direction in which the tensions evolve in order to predict future conflict events. The DL methodology adopted to the experimental conflict event model, is a Long-Short Term Memory (LSTM) Cell Recurrent Neural Network (RNN). LSTM models are well suited to classify, process, and make predictions based on time series data and forecast near-future events (Hochreiter & Schmidhuber, 1997; Chung et al., 2014).

By applying this model to conflict prediction, our implicit assumption is that the current situation depends on the conflict history. We could think of it as a composite function in which the oldest events are nested within the more recent events.

Mathematically speaking, past events receive in this way a smaller weight than the more recent events. To avoid this, and to equally 'reweight' all events in the model's memory, we apply the LSTM to our RNN.

In the same way a linear regression model is solved through an optimization problem of minimizing the squared errors between the prediction and the actual value of a dependent variable, the LSTM RNN is an optimization of a gradient while minimizing the model's errors.

Neural networks like LSTM RNNs are able to almost seamlessly model problems with multiple input variables and as mentioned by Sak et al. (2014), *"LSTM is a specific recurrent neural network (RNN) architecture that was designed to model temporal sequences and their long-range dependencies more accurately than conventional RNNs"* (Sak, Senior & Beaufays, 2014).

As previously said, LSTM RNNs are appropriate to classify, process, and make predictions based on time series data, since there can be lags of unknown duration between important events in a time series. This is a great benefit in time series forecasting and supervised time series learning (Bakker, 2002), areas in which classical linear methods fail to adapt to multivariate or multiple input forecasting problems.

Taking into account the update frequency of both the GDELT and the ICEWS datasets, we have aggregated the data by month for both datasets to be able to compare the results of the probability estimates of a conflict event for the same period. Next, we transformed the absolute number of articles of each major category and QuadClass into proportion of the total number of articles. We consider as independent variables all the 20 major categories and the 4 QuadClasses as defined in the CAMEO and applied on the GGELT and ICEWS datasets. By doing so, we provided as input to the model 24 independent variables as time-month records per country.

We have filtered the GDELT dataset to include only the available information after 1989, which is the starting year of the original GCRI input values, enabling a comparative analysis of the results obtained in the respective models.

In a fourth step, we create our model by using a random sample consisting out of 50% of the available dataset as a training set and the remaining 50% as the testing/controlling one. Having a testing and a training sample makes it possible to control and validate the accuracy of the model. We define the LSTM model with 50 neurons in the first hidden layer and with 1 neuron in the output layer for predicting the risk. The model consists of 191 separate models, one per each country included in the analysis. We then use the Root Mean Square Error (RMSE) to validate the accuracy of the model[2]. The model will be fit for 500 training epochs with a batch size of 72.

3.2 Conflict Risk Alarm System (CRA-S) Configuration

Through the DL model's capacity to predict the future proportion of conflict or cooperation related events in a country, we have set up a Conflict Risk Alarm System (CRA-S). The CRA-S signals social unrest upheavals (an abnormal increase in the proportion of the Q_{4x}, Q_{4x+1}) or the media pressure variations (increase or decrease in the total number of events mentioned as Q_{1x}, Q_{2x}, Q_{3x} or Q_{4x}, where x stands for the point in time). This allows policy makers to implement short-term preventive actions to mitigate conflict exacerbations at an earlier stage of the conflict development cycle.

The CRA-S functions can be detailed as follows: First, we aggregate the events recorded in each of the two databases per month. Next, we compute the monthly amount of news

[2] The root mean square error (RMSE) has been widely used as a standard statistical metric to measure model performance in various studies (Chai, Chai & Draxler, 2014). In order to validate the accuracy of the model we lagged the dataset by a month, so the prediction refers to the last available month.

articles reported in each QuadClass (Q_1, Q_2, Q_3, and Q_4) with respect to the total number of articles per month. Finally, we compute a 95% Confidence Interval (CI) to estimate the significance of the local maxima in the increase of the total number of events. The CI was computed setting a 3 and 6-month moving window. In the case of a 3-month moving window, we only take the events of the past 3 months into consideration to calculate the local maxima in conflict events and the CI.

The calculation of different time windows gives the opportunity to evaluate the predictions performance under different timeframes (see results in 4.2). Doing so, we can have an alarm for the cases in which the prediction of our model is out of the bound of the 95% CI, which means that the prediction is a real local max and the increase in the tension in a given country is significant.

3.3 Ranking of Countries based on CRA-S

In order to rank the countries in the most appropriate way, we compute the rate of change between the Q_4 of the current month and the Q_4 of the previous one (here called delta classification). Hence, the rate of change is

$$\Delta Q_4 = \frac{Q_{4x} - Q_{4x-1}}{Q_{4x-1}}$$

where Q_{4x} is the proportion of the Q_4 for the current month and Q_{4x-1} is the proportion of the Q_4 for the previous month. Based on this rate, we rank the countries so as the country with the highest increase in the Q_4 (ΔQ_4) will be first and the country with the highest decrease will be the last. In case the Q_{4x} is a local max, meaning that the increase in the current value of the Q_4 is significant, we have set an alarm following the same methodology as described in the section 3.2.

To the initial country ranking, we further add a set alarms (value 0 or 1 if true) that consist of the following parameters:

- **Alarm 1:** The proportion of the Q_4 (Q_{4x}) for the current month is a local max, meaning that the increase is significant and out of the 95% CI that we have calculated for the x-month moving window.
- **Alarm 2:** The total absolute number of the events mentioned (current values) is a local max.
- **Alarm 3:** The proportion of the predicted values of the Q_4 (Q_{4x+1}) for the next month is a local max.

Using these parameters, we re-rank the countries according to the following rules:

- **Initial ranking:** The initial ranking is based on the ΔQ_4.
- **Rule 1:** If all thee alarms in a country signal at the same time, this country will be re-ranked as first. In case there is more than one country, we keep the delta classification from the initial ranking.
- **Rule 2:** If two of the alarms in a country signal at the same time, this country will be re-ranked just after the countries that have three alarm signals. In case there is more than one country, we keep the delta classification from the initial ranking.
- **Rule 3:** If one of the alarms in a country signals, that country will be re-ranked just after the countries that have two alarm signals. In case there is more than one country, we keep the delta classification.
- **Rule 4:** The remaining countries with no alarm signals are ranked thereafter by keeping their initial ranking (ΔQ_4).

Taking into account the presence or absence of the abovementioned alarms reflecting different time windows the analyst has a choice in either summarising the news, having long term predictions or a more detailed overview of the situation. As a result, we create a classification method based on a system of three different alarms, taking into account both the absolute and the relative number of events per country.

4. Results

4.1 Deep Learning Root Mean Square Error (RMSE) and Model Predictions

The results of running the LSTM RNN model for five study cases and two databases are listed in the last column of Table 1 for March 2019. To see how accurate our model predictions are in estimating the percentage of material conflict events (Q_4 of the CAMEO classification) in percentage of the overall events, we measure the Root Mean Square Error (RMSE)[3] of the model, which is the standard deviation of the residuals (prediction errors).

Country	Dataset	RMSE
Libya	ICEWS	0.215
	GDELT	0.089
Sudan	ICEWS	0.097
	GDELT	0.041
Egypt	ICEWS	0.119
	GDELT	0.059
Maldives	ICEWS	0.210
	GDELT	0.071
Nicaragua	ICEWS	0.147
	GDELT	0.063

[3] RMSE is a measure of how spread out the residuals are. In other words, it tells you how concentrated the data is around the line of best fit.

Table 1: RMSE for March 2019 per dataset

As reported in Table 1, the RMSE using the GDELT data is the lowest in all the case studies. In other words, the predictions based on this dataset are closer to the observed values. We postulate that due to the limited data availability (1995-2019) in the ICEWS database, the model using the GDELT data is more precise and accurate.

4.2 Early Warning Alarm System Predictions and Accuracy

In this part of the paper, the results of the early warning alarm system (an abnormal increase in the proportion of Q_4 – material conflict events) are presented for five case study scenarios and two databases. As we described above, an alarm is given in case there is an extraordinary increase in the predictions out of the 95% CI we have set for two local maxima in respectively a 3-month and a 6-month window from the case study event.

In Table 2, we report whether or not the model gives us an alarm for the Arab spring in Libya and Egypt, the Sudanese protests, the political crisis in the Maldives in 2018, and the Nicaraguan protests the same year. For this experiment, we have pre-filtered the GDELT dataset in order to obtain more reliable input data. Based on our GDELT validation (Halkia et al. 2019), we have set a filter on 100 mentions per article. In other words, when the filter is applied, only articles that have been mentioned more than 100 times are included in that part of the analysis (GDELT100 in Table 2). This has been done to remove information noise in the GDELT database, hypothesizing that if an event really happens, it should be reproduced by more than one media source and in more than one article. We are aware that this may lead to the exclusion of important information in countries where local press is being repressed and international media has only a limited interest. However, the inclusion of all available information within the GDELT database affects significantly the results[4].

ISO3	Date	Dataset	3-month local max	6-month local max
LBY	Feb 2011	GDELT	**ALARM**	**ALARM**
		GDELT100	**ALARM**	**ALARM**
		ICEWS	NO ALARM	NO ALARM
SDN	Dec 2018	GDELT	NO ALARM	NO ALARM
		GDELT100	**ALARM**	**ALARM**
		ICEWS	NO ALARM	NO ALARM
EGY	Jan 2011	GDELT	NO ALARM	NO ALARM
		GDELT100	**ALARM**	**ALARM**
		ICEWS	NO ALARM	NO ALARM
MDV	Feb 2018	GDELT	NO ALARM	NO ALARM
		GDELT100	NO ALARM	NO ALARM
		ICEWS	NO ALARM	NO ALARM
NIC	Apr 2018	GDELT	NO ALARM	NO ALARM
		GDELT100	NO ALARM	NO ALARM
		ICEWS	**ALARM**	**ALARM**

Table 2: Sample validation of the predictions based on past events.

In Table 2, we can observe that the ALARM rang for Libya's Arab Spring using the GDELT dataset (either filtered or unfiltered), while the model predicted the 2018-19 Sudanese protests and the Start of Arab spring in Egypt using the filtered GDELT data. In contrast, the ICEWS dataset could only predict the 2018–2019 Nicaraguan protests. Overall, using the filter improves the reliability of the GDELT database and enhances the model towards more accurate predictions. In addition, the 3-month and 6-month window estimations render similar predictions, demonstrating that both time frames report equal results.

5. Discussion

In this paper, the experimental conflict event model, which is based on country-level actor-based event data, signalling a potential trigger (including demonstrations, strikes, election violence, etc.) to violent conflict, has been discussed, along with its present shortcomings.

The experiment presented here, using an LSTM RNN model to predict the materialization of a conflict, demonstrates that the GDELT is potentially the most comprehensive database, probably due to the amount of available information, despite all its limitations, including information noise. However, in some cases (islands and small countries), where the reporting is limited, social upheaval prediction may be challenging.

Nevertheless, many provisions must be added to any method using the GDELT database in order to render it accurate and effective. The LSTM RNN model we propose, one of the most advanced neural networks for modelling temporal sequences and their long-range dependencies, performs well and is able to handle time series data and classify each event based on historical information. While the absolute number of events informs of a significant escalation or de-escalation of tension in a given country, the normalized number of events provides information on the relative significance of the occurrence to preceding ones. The proportions taken by different types of events complete the picture on how a conflict is escalating,

[4] We are not able to do the same filtering for ICEWS due to dataset limitations (no available URL).

stagnating or de-escalating from month to month. Finally, the local maxima modelling gives us the possibility to have an early warning system, which informs the policy makers in case of an abnormal increase in the tensions in a given country.

The results indicate that the model is able to correctly predict social upheaval in countries where there is available information on news (Libya, Sudan, Egypt). In contrast, for the cases where there is very little or no available information (Nicaragua, Maldives), the model fails to detect upheavals. The next steps to further evaluate the performance and robustness of the model will consider a k-fold cross validation and an ANOVA (ANalysis Of Variances) analysis.

6. Conclusions

This paper presented the data driven limitations of the experimental conflict event model, developed at the Joint Research Centre of the European Commission.

The proposed model integrates and identifies every stage of the conflict development or de-escalation in its entire complexity, including internationalized contentious action. Using country-level actor-based event datasets that signal potential triggers to violent conflict such as demonstrations, strikes, or elections-related violence, the model aims at estimating the occurrence of material conflict events, under the assumption that an increase in material conflict events goes along with a decrease in material and verbal cooperation.

The DL methodology used to model the conflict events is a Long-Short Term Memory (LSTM) Cell Recurrent Neural Network (RNN). These models are well-suited to classify, process and make predictions based on time series data and forecast near future events. Besides this DL model, we have set up an early warning alarm system to signal abnormal social unrest upheavals.

Two potential datasets and their limitations, that follow the CAMEO political event coding classification, were discussed in this paper: (i) the Global Data on Events Location and Tone (GDELT) project and (ii) the Integrated Crisis Early Warning System (ICEWS) Dataverse dataset.

Even though the DL and early warning alarm seem to be able to predict the materialization of a conflict in the near future, the analysis of the results conveys that implementing the GDELT or ICEWS as an input to the experimental conflict event model requires overcoming certain obstacles. Firstly, the automated codebook algorithm is not publicly available for GDELT, which does not allow investigation on the source of potential errors in the news classification. Secondly, the ICEWS data sources are not publicly available, so validation is not facilitated. Common issues need to be resolved in both datasets: false positive rates, duplication rates, geographical or socioeconomic biases, "media fatigue", particularly in conflict zones.

The Europe Media Monitor (EMM) event dataset could be a promising alternative in the near future, but it could not be tested at this stage, because it is not based on the CAMEO classification methods. The Political Language Ontology for Verifiable Event Records (PLOVER) dictionary could replace the existing CAMEO codebook and provide new categories such as elections. However, it is not available yet. A new automated codebook algorithm could be a potential solution to overcome both obstacles created to the GDELT dataset and the present classifiers.

To conclude, the experimental conflict event modelling methodology applied on the GDELT dataset presently gives policy makers the possibility to observe on escalating or de-escalating situations in a country on a monthly basis. However, event-based systems will require supplementary research to offset the databases' shortcomings, such as automated data validation, new classifiers and dictionaries reflecting the changing nature of conflict and most importantly evidence on the pathways between social unrest and violent conflict.

7. Bibliographical References

Alikhani, Ehsan (2014) *Computational Social Analysis: Social Unrest Prediction Using Textual Analysis of News* (https://www.bps.go.id/dynamictable/2018/05/18/1337/persentase-panjang-jalan-tol-yang-beroperasi-menurut-operatornya-2014.html).

Bakker, Bram (2002) Reinforcement Learning Memory. *International Conference on Neural Information Processing Systems* 1475–1482 (https://papers.nips.cc/paper/1953-reinforcement-learning-with-long-short-term-memory.pdf).

Chai, Tianfeng, T Chai & RR Draxler (2014) Root mean square error (RMSE) or mean absolute error (MAE)?-Arguments against avoiding RMSE in the literature. *Geosci. Model Dev* 7: 1247–1250 (www.geosci-model-dev.net/7/1247/2014/).

Chung, Junyoung, Caglar Gulcehre, KyungHyun Cho & Yoshua Bengio (2014) Empirical Evaluation of Gated Recurrent Neural Networks on Sequence Modeling. 1–9 (http://arxiv.org/abs/1412.3555).

GDELT (2019) The GDELT Project (https://www.gdeltproject.org/).

Halkia, Matina, Stefano Ferri, Inès Joubert-Boitat & Francesca Saporiti (2017a) *Conflict Risk Indicators: Significance and Data Management in the GCRI.* Luxembourg: Publications Office of the European

Union.

Halkia, Matina, Stefano Ferri, Inès Joubert-Boitat, Francesca Saporiti & Mayeul Kauffmann (2017b) *The Global Conflict Risk Index (GCRI) Regression Model : Data Ingestion , Processing , and Output Methods*. Luxembourg: Publications Office of the European Union.

Halkia, Matina, Stefano Ferri, Michail Papazoglou, Marie-sophie VaN Damme, Gabriel Jenkinson, Kathrin-Manuela Baumann & Dimitrios Thomakos (2019) *Dynamic Global Conflict Risk Index*.

Halkia, Matina, Stefano Ferri, Marie K Schellens, Michail Papazoglou & Dimitrios Thomakos (2020) The Global Conflict Risk Index: A quantitative tool for policy support on conflict prevention. *Progress in Disaster Science* (March): 100069 (https://linkinghub.elsevier.com/retrieve/pii/S2590061720300065).

Hegre, Håvard, Joakim Karlsen, Håvard Mokleiv Nygård, Håvard Strand & Henrik Urdal (2013) Predicting Armed Conflict , 2010 – 2050. *International Studies Quarterly* 57(2): 250–270.

Hochreiter, Sepp & Jurgen Schmidhuber (1997) Long short-term memory. *Neural Computation* 9(8): 1735–1780.

ICEWS | Lockheed Martin (2019) (https://www.lockheedmartin.com/en-us/capabilities/research-labs/advanced-technology-labs/icews.html#MoreInfo).

Levin, Noam, Saleem Ali & David Crandall (2018) Utilizing remote sensing and big data to quantify conflict intensity: The Arab Spring as a case study. *Applied Geography* 94(May): 1–17.

Qiao, Fengcai, Pei Li, Xin Zhang, Zhaoyun Ding, Jiajun Cheng & Hui Wang (2017) Predicting Social Unrest Events with Hidden Markov Models Using GDELT. *Discrete Dynamics in Nature and Society* (https://doi.org/10.1155/2017/8180272).

Sak, Hasim, Andrew Senior & Francoise Beaufays (2014) *Long Short-Term Memory Recurrent Neural Network Architectures for Large Scale Acoustic Modeling*.

Schrodt, Philip A (2012) *CAMEO Event* (http://eventdata.psu.edu/).

Schrodt, Philip A & David Van Brackle (2013) Automated Coding of Political Event Data. In: *Handbook of Computational Approaches to Counterterrorism*. New York, NY: Springer New York, 23–49 (http://link.springer.com/10.1007/978-1-4614-5311-6_2).

Smith, Emmanuel M, Jim Smith, Phil Legg & Simon Francis (2018) Predicting the Occurrence of World News Events Using Recurrent Neural Networks and Auto-Regressive Moving Average Models. *Advances in Intelligent Systems and Computing* 650(MI): 191–202.

Szayna, Thomas, Stephen Watts, Angela O'Mahony, Bryan Frederick & Jennifer Kavanagh (2017) What Are the Trends in Armed Conflicts, and What Do They Mean for U.S. Defense Policy? (https://www.rand.org/pubs/research_reports/RR1904.html).

Tikuisis, Peter, David Carment & Yiagadeesen Samy (2013) *Prediction of Intrastate Conflict Using State Structural Factors and Events Data. Journal of Conflict Resolution* Vol. 57.

Wang, Wei, Ryan Kennedy, David Lazer & Naren Ramakrishnan (2016) Growing pains for global monitoring of societal events. Automated event coding raises promise and concerns. *Science* 353(6307): 1502–1504.

Ward, Michael D, Andreas Beger, Josh Cutler, Matthew Dickenson, Cassy Dorff & Ben Radford (2013) *Comparing GDELT and ICEWS Event Data. Analysis* Vol. 21 (http://mdwardlab.com/biblio/comparing-gdelt-and-icews-event-data).

Yonamine, James E (2013) *Predicting Future Levels of Violence in Afghanistan Districts. The 3rd Annual Meeting Of The European Political Science Association* (http://jayyonamine.com/wp-content/uploads/2013/03/Forecasting_Afghanistan.pdf).

Proceedings of AESPEN 2020, pages 49–56
Language Resources and Evaluation Conference (LREC 2020), Marseille, 11–16 May 2020

Supervised Event Coding from Text Written in Arabic: Introducing Hadath

Javier Osorio,[1] Alejandro Reyes,[2] Alejandro Beltran,[1] Atal Ahmadzai[1]

[1]University of Arizona, [2]AUDI Mexico,
School of Government and Public Policy, University of Arizona, United States
Corresponding author: josorio1@email.arizona.edu

Abstract

This article introduces Hadath, a supervised protocol for coding event data from text written in Arabic. Hadath contributes to recent efforts in advancing multi-language event coding using computer-based solutions. In this application, we focus on extracting event data about the conflict in Afghanistan from 2008 to 2018 using Arabic information sources. The implementation relies first on a Machine Learning algorithm to classify news stories relevant to the Afghan conflict. Then, using Hadath, we implement the Natural Language Processing component for event coding from Arabic script. The output database contains daily geo-referenced information at the district level on who did what to whom, when and where in the Afghan conflict. The data helps to identify trends in the dynamics of violence, the provision of governance, and traditional conflict resolution in Afghanistan for different actors over time and across space.

Keywords: event data, information extraction, Arabic, Afghanistan, conflict

1. Introduction

Over the last few years, collaborative work between Political Scientists and Computer Scientists produced considerable contributions to understanding socio-political conflict processes around the world thanks to the production of computerized event data (Althaus et al., 2019; Bond et al., 2003; Hürriyetoğlu et al., 2019; Mohiuddin et al., 2016; O'Brien, 2012; Schrodt et al., 2014; Schrodt, 2012; Subrahmanian, 2013; Wang et al., 2016). These event coding projects take advantage of the vast availability of online news reports to extract information about *who did what to whom, where, and when*, thus producing a wealth of data about incidents of socio-political conflict around the world. Despite the enormous contributions of these research projects, the large majority of these projects primarily use text written in English as their source of information.

Unfortunately, coding socio-political incidents of conflict in foreign locations where English is not a native language using text written in English is likely to generate discrepancies that affect the quality of the data output. To address this Anglo-centric approach, in recent years, a handful of research projects started engaging in multi-lingual event coding. Some of these efforts rely on automated translation from non-English text into English (Boschee et al., 2016), while other code event data directly from text written in non-English languages (Schrodt et al., 2014; Osorio and Reyes, 2017; Osorio et al., 2019b).

In line with ongoing research advancing multi-lingual event coding, this article introduces Hadath, a supervised protocol for coding event data from text written in Modern Standard Arabic. At its core, Hadath uses shallow parsing to identify events in the corpus based on entries provided by dictionaries of actors, actions, and locations. In this way, Hadath follows other sparse coding protocols (Schrodt, 2009) while contributing to pioneering work of computerized event coding from Arabic text (Open Event Data Alliance, 2016; Halterman et al., 2018).

This application focuses on extracting event data about the Afghan conflict between 2008 and 2018 using narratives from Arabic newspapers. Following the literature on wartime order and rebel governance (Arjona, 2016; Staniland, 2012), our conceptualization of event data in the Afghan conflict includes acts of violence, as well as the provision of governance, and traditional conflict resolution. This helps moving beyond a narrow focus on violence and including other non-violent behaviors taking place in conflict settings. The methodology consists of two main steps. First, we deploy a Machine Learning (ML) classifier to identify the specific news stories relevant to the Afghan conflict from a vast collection of news articles written in Arabic. Second, we rely on Hadath to implement a Natural Language Processing (NLP) protocol for event coding. The resulting database presents geo-referenced information at the daily district level on who did what to whom, when, and where in the Afghan conflict.

2. Recent Developments

2.1. NLP tools in Arabic

Although English is the dominant language in NLP processing tools, in recent years, scholars have been advancing non-English NLP developments including tools for Modern Standard Arabic. These emerging resources in Arabic include news articles corpora such as *i*ArabicWeb16 (Suwaileh et al., 2016; Khaled Yasser and Elsayed, 2018); annotation of social media in Arabic through the EveTAR and ArSAS projects (Hasanain et al., 2018; AbdelRahim Elmadany and Magdy, 2018); tools to identify dialects and regional variations in Arabic (Zaghouani and Charfi, 2018; Alshutayri and Atwell, 2018); and lexical disambiguation resources for Arabic diacritics (Sawsan Alqahtani and Zaghouani, 2018).

In line with these developments, the field of computerized event coding has been advancing tools for processing text written in Arabic. The Open Event Data Alliance (OEDA) is adapting Universal PETRARCH for coding event data from Arabic using the CAMEO ontology (Open Event

Data Alliance, 2016; Gerner et al., 2002). As part of this project, OEDA developed a supervised tool for translating CAMEO dictionaries from English to Arabic (Halterman et al., 2018). Hadath contributes to these efforts to developing event coding capabilities for Arabic text.

2.2. Text-as-Data in Conflict Studies

The use of text-as-data is developing solid roots in the social sciences (Grimmer and Steward, 2013). Researchers in political science and public administration are rapidly catalyzing the leverage of computerized text analysis by exploring previously uncharted domains of inquiry and developing increasingly sophisticated text analysis tools (Wilkerson and Casas, 2017; Hollibaugh, 2018).

The use of computerized event data revolutionized the way in which researchers analyze conflict processes. Traditionally, the field primarily relied on manually coded databases of conflict processes around the world such as the Uppsala Conflict Data Program (UCDP) (Sundberg and Melander, 2013) and the Armed Conflict and Event Dataset (ACLED) (Raleigh et al., 2010). In contrast with these manually coded databases, some scholars took advantage of NLP tools and the vast availability of online news articles to develop computerized event coding protocols.

The pioneering work of Schrodt opened the door to machine-generated event data from news papers through the KEDS program (Schrodt, 1998). After developing TABARI, a second generation coder based on sparse parsing, Schrodt triggered an enormous production of event data (Schrodt, 2009). The third generation of coders is PETRARCH, which incorporates full parsing and Treebanks (Schrodt et al., 2014). Parallel to these projects, the Integrated Crisis Early Warning System (ICEWS) program (O'Brien, 2010) advanced its own event coding tools.

In addition to these main programs, the field of computerized event coding in conflict studies is now populated with a variety of data generation approaches of increasing coverage, sophistication, and accuracy (Althaus et al., 2019; Bond et al., 2003; Halterman et al., 2018; Hammond and Weidmann, 2014a; Hürriyetoğlu et al., 2019; Subrahmanian, 2013; Osorio and Reyes, 2017; Osorio et al., 2019a). With a few exceptions (Osorio and Reyes, 2017; Piskorski et al., 2011), most protocols almost exclusively rely on news stories written in English, thus neglecting the richness and detail of vast amounts of information produced in foreign locations in their native languages. The field is barely opening to the possibility of processing text in non-English languages for event coding. To advance this potential, the Open Event Data Alliance has been spearheading research enabling the generation of event data in Arabic (Open Event Data Alliance, 2016; Halterman et al., 2018). Hadath contributes to these recent research endeavors to process Modern Standard Arabic for event coding.

3. Conflict in Afghanistan

The current insurgency in Afghanistan is the continuation of a decades-long warfare in the country. Starting with the invasion of the Soviet Union in late 1970s, followed by the civil war of the 1990s, and then confounded by the emergence of the Taliban in 1996, the war in Afghanistan has a long history and multiple actors. However, the roots of the current Taliban insurgency go back to late 2001 when the U.S. led international coalition forces toppled the Taliban's Emirates of Afghanistan (CFR, 2020). This intervention was in response to the 9/11 terrorist attacks that Al-Qaeda carried out in the U.S. Though, the Emirates of the Taliban were not directly involved in conducting the attacks, they provided sanctuaries and safe havens for the leadership and strategic infrastructure of Al-Qaeda in Afghanistan (Kean, 2011). Using Afghanistan as its base, the Al-Qaeda organization coordinated the 9/11 suicide attacks in the U.S.

After being defeated by the U.S. military intervention, the Taliban re-emerged as an armed insurgency against the newly establish Afghan government and the international forces in 2003 (Kenneth and Thomas, 2017). The resurgence, which started with scattered run and hit attacks in different remote parts of the country, has systematically grown both in magnitude and geographic scope in the subsequent years. By 2006, the scattered attacks had developed to a full-fledged insurgency in different parts of the country (Jones, 2008). In addition, The Taliban also strategically included different methods of inflicting targeted and indiscriminate violence including suicide bombings, implanting Improvised Explosive Devices (IEDs), and conducting well-coordinated military attacks against strategic targets.

4. Text Gathering and Classification

4.1. Gathering News Stories

As part of a larger research project funded by the United States Department of Defense - Minerva Research Initiative (71623-LS-MRI), this paper focuses on the Afghan conflict to test Hadath. Although Dari and Pashto are the official languages in Afghanistan, these languages are still part of the Arab sign-language family, which is common to several languages in Asia, Africa, and the Middle East. Since there are more resources available to the researchers in terms of text, NLP tools, and human coders in Arabic than in Dari or Pashto, we developed first the capacity to code event data in Arabic as a practical matter. Having a functional software for event coding in Arabic serves as the "possible adjacent" (Jhonson, 2011) that can be extended to other Arabic script languages, including Dari and Pashto.

To generate this collection of news articles written in Arabic, we relied on the Nexis Uni global news platform, an online repository hosting vast collections of newspapers in different languages. Nexis Uni contains 17 different newspapers published in Arabic with over 2.5 million articles collected between 2008 and 2018. To gather relevant news stories, we ran a robust query in Nexis Uni's search engine to identify articles potentially related to the conflict in Afghanistan. A team of three research assistants manually downloaded all the articles that the search output produced. This text gathering effort generated a collection of 100,857 individual stories.

For Hadath to identify the day in which an event occurred, the filename of each article must incorporate its date of publication. To enable this feature, we used the *date_extractor* Python package (Dufour, 2020) to identify the publication date, and then used this information to modify the file name of each news story so that it indicates the date of publication. This process facilitates grouping news stories in year-specific folders that served to build the training data corpus described in the section below.

4.2. Machine Learning Classifier

The Nexis Uni search engine returned several news articles not directly relevant to our selection criteria. Although the query included *boolean* exclusions to filter out unrelated stories, a considerable portion of the retrieved articles were tangential to our study.

To resolve this ambiguity, we initially tasked a team of 6 human coders to manually classify each article. Each coder was randomly assigned to a folder from which they briefly read each article and coded as "accept" or "exclude." Coders classified the stories based on a direct reference to a conflict-related incident occurring within Afghanistan. To "accept" an article, the story must include a description of an actual event or incident related to any of the three dimensions of interest: acts of violence, provision of governance in the context of war, or traditional conflict mitigation. The most challenging aspect of this task is identifying relevant news stories that explicitly report on factual incidents of events occurring in the country, not just opinions or broad discussion loosely related to Afghanistan. In consequence, we excluded statements or opinions made by foreign persons or entities about Afghanistan and other international reports summarizing the conflict.

To asses the reliability of our human coders, the 6 coders applied the same classification routine to a random sample of 1,000 articles and we evaluated their agreement. This revealed that three coders were producing unreliable classifications. To resolve this issue we utilized a Machine Learning (ML) text classifier model described below, trained on the tags assigned by the coders with the highest agreement. The Fleiss' Kappa for these three coders reached .817 and a paired inter-coder agreement averaged of 92%. Given this assessment of inter-coder reliability, we used their initial classification on the universe of articles as training data.

The resulting training data consists of 55,870 articles that contain no explicit biases in classification. This includes 17,426 articles tagged as "accept," and 38,444 classified as "exclude". Although the categories are unbalanced, we decided against balancing the data because we expect the universe of observations to follow the same distribution.

The classification pipeline first normalized the text and removed any English language characters, digits and stop words. The light stemming feature of the *Tashaphyne* python package (Zerrouki, 2012) served to reduce words to their stem. We used *TfidfVectorizer* from *sci-kit learn* (Pedregosa et al., 2011) to convert the Arabic characters into a features matrix based on the recurrence of relevant words, with the maximum number of features capped at 5,000.

To improve the accuracy of the training data and to resolve ambiguities between human coders and the machine, we trained a Logistic Regression (LR) that reported an F1 of 0.87 and used the parameters from this model to classify the training data. This process generated 3,929 articles where the human coder and model were in disagreement. Three human coders focused on resolving these ambiguities by correctly classifying each article. This subset only represents 7% of the training data but it greatly improved model performance. This step modified the number of articles in the "accept" category to 16,339.

We evaluate the performance of each model using k-fold cross-validation (CV) that shuffles and splits the data into 5 subsets, and leaves out 10% for validation. Figure 1 shows the average F1 performance for each models. We used a random grid search to evaluate different Convolutional Neural Network (CNN) specifications and reported the two best performing parameters. CNN 1 and CNN 2 share a vocabulary of 150,166, 128 filters and an embedding dimension of 50. CNN 1 has a kernel size of 3 and averaged an F1 of 0.923, in contrast CNN 2 has a kernel size of 5 and averaged an F1 of 0.922. The Random Forest (RF) model averaged 0.924 F1. The Multinomial Naive Bayes (NB) model averaged 0.835 F1. The Extreme Gradient Boosting (XGB) model averaged 0.919 F1. The linear Support Vector Machine (SVM) classifier averaged 0.94 F1. Using this updated training data, the LR model performance increased to 0.94 F1. To decide between LR and SVM, we re-trained the model using the entire training data rather than the k-fold CV approach, and left out 10% of the data for testing. This process resulted in an F1 of 0.934 for SVM and an F1 of 0.938 for LR. Given the slightly better performance of the latter, we use LR to classify the universe of articles.

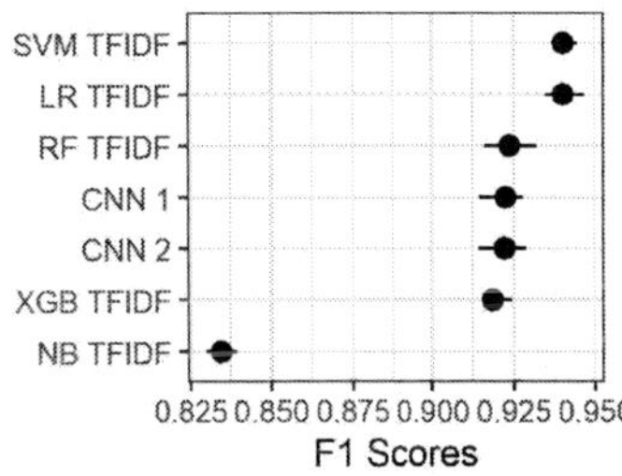

Figure 1: Machine Learning models

For the collection of 100,857 articles, we normalized and processed them following the same procedure implemented for the training data. Then we applied the parameters of the LR model to classify the entire collection, which resulted in a classification of 26,235 relevant articles.

5. Event Coding

5.1. Introducing Hadath

After selecting the relevant news stories, the next step is to extract events from the text collected. For this task we developed Hadath, a supervised NLP application for extracting events and their geographic location from text in Arabic. Hadath stems from a long tradition of coders using sparse parsing to extract event data. The first of these programs used to collect conflict data was Tabari (Schrodt, 2009). This software served as the source code or inspiration for a long line of coders in the social sciences (Best et al., 2013; Hammond and Weidmann, 2014b; Chojnacki et al., 2012; Schrodt, 2001; Schrodt et al., 2004; Schrodt, 2006; Schrodt et al., 2014; Schrodt and Gerner, 2012)

An event can be defined as the categorical description of someone doing something to someone else, at a specific time and location based on the explicit information contained in text. Event data contains five components: a **source** performing an action, the **action** observed, and the **target** of the observed action, a specific **date**, and an identifiable geographic **location**. Hadath is capable of extracting all five features from text in Arabic, and to the extent of our knowledge is the first program with these capabilities.

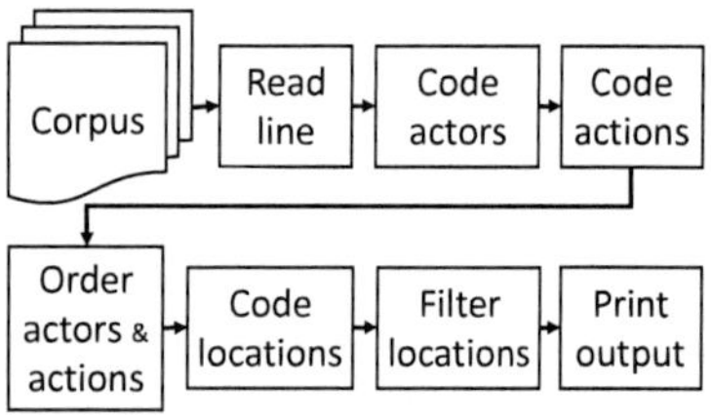

Figure 2: Hadath system

Figure 2 presents the Hadath algorithm:

1. **Read the text**. Take the Arabic corpus as an input file. The corpus contains a unique identifier per news article and for each paragraph within each news story. Paragraphs are formatted as a long line reading from right to left. Hadath uses the line as the coding unit.

2. **Coding actors**. Load the dictionary of actors containing named entities used as search criteria. Each entry has an associated numeric code. Search for those entities in the corpus, looking first for the longest names.[1] Record each entry in textual and numeric format for every match between the dictionary and the corpus.

3. **Coding actions**. Load the actions dictionary containing verb phrases. Use those entries as search criteria for detecting actions. Record the actions in the same way it does with the actors.

4. **Ordering actors and actions**. After finishing coding actors and verbs in each line, reorder the coding output according to the order in which actors and actions appear in the script (from right to left).

5. **Code locations**. For each paragraph with a matching actor or action, use the locations dictionaries to look for the provinces (states) and districts (counties) mentioned in the corpus. Save the matching locations.

6. **Filter locations**. To minimize the problem of geographic ambiguity, use the locations filter to discard false positives for geographic locations.

7. **Print output**. Print the output indicating first the date of the event, the matching actors an actions in the order they appear in the text, print any matching locations.

[1]Prioritizing long strings improves the coding efficient by not devoting resources looking for shorter words or sub-strings.

For this application, we use the corpus of articles on Afghanistan discussed in the previous section. This collection contains news articles in Arabic script related to the Afghan conflict from 2008 through 2018. The text was preprocessed and reformatted, producing a corpus with about 90 MB of text across 394,690 sentences.
The dictionary of actors used in this implementation contains 318 named entities in Arabic related to organizations or individuals including the main insurgent groups, coalition forces, international and local actors relevant to the Afghan conflict. This list is based on knowledge of the case, available list of relevant actors made by country experts, and the discovery of additional actors identified using Named Entity Recognition (NER) (Abdelali et al., 2016). Table 1 below reports the main actor categories.

Table 1: Main Categories of Actors

Domestic Armed Actor	**Civil Society**
Afghan Taliban	Civilians
Warlords (Mujahideen)	Ethnic
Other	Religious
Int. Armed Actors	Women
Al-Qaeda	**Local organizations**
Hamas	Educational
Hezbollah	Private sector
Int. Jihadi Groups	Political organizations
ISIS	Political Parties
Muslim Brotherhood	Other
Int. Security Forces	**Int. Actors**
ISAF	Foreign governments
US	Multilateral Organizations
Other	International NGOs
National Security Forces	Political Parties
Army	Private Corporations
Intelligence	**State**
Police	Executive
	Judicial
	Legislative

The actions dictionary comprises 4,694 Arabic verb phrases associated with violence, governance provision, or traditional conflict resolution. The verbs used in this dictionary omit pronunciation diacritics, thus leaving plain Arabic script. This required deduplicating different verb conjugations that end up with the same plain Arabic script after removing diacritics. Table 2 shows the three main categories considered in the study: Violence, Governance, and Pashtoonwali (traditional lifestyle). To build this dictionary, we first applied Part of Speech (POS) tagging on the corpus to generate an initial list of verbs. Human coders then filtered them out based based on their relevance to the Afghan conflict. Coders then added variations and synonyms of each verb to build up redundancy, which is necessary for unstructured text. To do so, we used online web resources to consider all possible verb conjugations.
To geo-reference events, Hadath uses the dictionaries of Provinces (equivalent to states) and Districts (equivalent to

Table 2: Main Action Categories

Violence	Governance
Physical violence Economic extortion	Judicial governance Policing
Pashtoonwali	Taxation
Conflict mitigation Reconciliation	

counties) to identify the location of the event. The dictionaries comprise all 34 provinces and 400 districts of Afghanistan, including variations on Province and District spelling as well as potential abbreviations.

To reduce the risk of false positives in the identification of locations, Hadath uses the locations filter to confirm that the location identified is in fact a physical location. For example, this dictionary contains nuances that Hadath uses to distinguish between Kabul street and the city of Kabul.

The final step consists of a post-coding process for cleaning the output, validating to asses performance, and removing duplicate events. The resulting output constitutes a geo-referenced database of event data throughout Afghanistan at the daily-district level between 2008 and 2018.

Below, we illustrate how Hadath uses dictionaries to identify events, actors, and locations in text. Consider an example where the actors dictionary includes the following two groups: the "Taliban" as `[10100]` طالبان and "NATO soldiers" as `[20100]` عساكر الناتو. In addition, the actions dictionary includes reference to the verb "attack" `[101]` هاجم. The locations dictionary may include the district of "Khanabad" `[1401]` خان آباد and the province of "Kunduz" `[14]` كونوز. Using a sparse parsing approach, Hadath searches through the corpus to identify explicit matches of these words within the text. Table 3 presents a basic coding example of text in Arabic followed by the numeric output that Hadath generates. The table also includes the English translation for the reader to follow.

Table 3: Hadath Coding Example

الطالبان هاجمت عساكر الناتو في الخان اباد بكونوز

`20100 101 10100 1401 14`

Taliban attacked NATO soldiers in Khanabad, Kunduz

In this example, Hadath would read from right to left the Arabic sentence and identify the "Taliban" (طالبان) and "NATO soldiers" (عساكر الناتو) as the relevant actors and assign the codes `10100` and `20100`, respectively. The program would also match on the verb "attacked" (هاجم) and record the code `101`. After confirming that the location names should not be filtered out, it would identify the district of "Khanabad" (خان آباد) as `1401` and the province of "Kunduz" (كونوز) as `14`. In this way, Hadath identifies event data.

6. Results

This section describes the event data that Hadath extracted from the collection of Arabic news stories on Afghanistan. To avoid artificial inflation of event data caused by multiple sources reporting the same event, we used the "one-per-day" rule and deduplicated events using a pipeline that reduces multiple mentions of the same event per day.

Overall, Hadath detected 17,614 actors in this coding exercise. Figure 3 shows the frequency of actor records by category. Results show that the Taliban is the most active armed group in the conflict with 16.8% of the total records. Other domestic armed groups like the Mujahideen warlords (with 3.7%) and international armed groups such as Al-Qaeda (with 5.5%) and the Islamic State of Iraq and Syria, ISIS (with 4.5%) are also present in Afghanistan, but their salience in the conflict is secondary when compared to the Taliban. In general, the combination of all domestic and international non-state armed actors amounts to 30.8% of the actors recorded in Afghanistan, which is indicative of the high degree of complexity of this conflict.

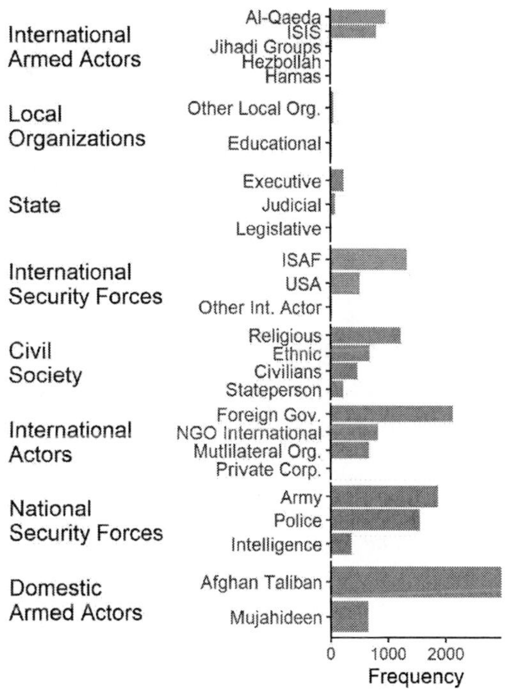

Figure 3: Frequency of Actors.

The data also reveals the central role of the Afghan security forces (with 21.4% of the total) as well as the international forces (with 10.5%) active in Afghanistan. It is noticeable, that the Afghan Army (10.6%) and the Police (8.8%) have a more active role than United States troops (2.9%) and International Security Assistance Forces, ISAF (7.6%). In general, the combined contribution of Afghan and international security forces amounts to 31.9% of the records. This share of the total detections is comparable to that of the insurgent organizations, which is indicative of the balance of forces and the high level of contestation in the Afghan conflict.

In addition to outlining the main contenders in the Afghan conflict, the data highlights the involvement of the international community (20.5% of the total) in Afghanistan. There is intense activity form foreign government representatives, diplomatic missions, international NGOs, and multilateral organizations. Finally, the data also is suggestive of the high degree of diversity in the Afghan civil society sector (14.7%) with the relevant presence of religious figures as well as representatives of different ethnic groups.
Figure 4 details the types of actions that Hadath identified in this coding exercise. In contrast to over-simplistic characterizations of the Afghan conflict, the data reveals the importance of Governance provision in the midst of war. In general, about 54.4% of the actions relate to the supply of Governance in the form of judicial services (18.4%), policing (19.9%), and taxation (16.1%). The second most relevant action category relates to the use of violence in the context of the armed conflict, with 28.6% of the records. As expected, the category of physical violence reports the highest proportion of incidents with 23.5% of all recorded actions. Acts of economic extortion amount to 5.1% of the cases. Finally, the data highlights the importance of traditional practices of conflict resolution and reconciliation at the community level (Pashtoonwali), which accounts for 17% of the data.

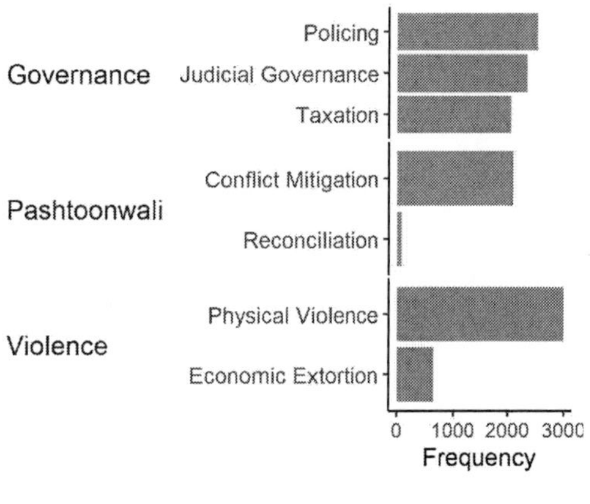

Figure 4: Frequency of Actions

Figure 5 presents the geo-location of events at the province level. As the graph indicates, the majority of incidents take place in the Helmand province and in Kandahar, which are well known hot-spots of conflict in Afghanistan.
Figure 6 showing the trends of actors over time. This graph helps to identify some insightful dynamics in the Afghan conflict. The first escalation of activity between 2008 and 2015 directly relates to the Taliban expansion from rural areas to populated urban centers such as Kabul, thus increasing its influence over the country (Masadykov et al., 2010). In addition, the Islamic State of of Iraq and Syria (ISIS or Daesh) emerged in Afghanistan around 2015 and expanded its activities to the Eastern regions of the country (Gambhir, 2015). The sharp decline in event detection in 2016 reflects the withdrawal of U.S. military personnel from Afghanistan in 2015 (CFR, 2020). Between 2011 and

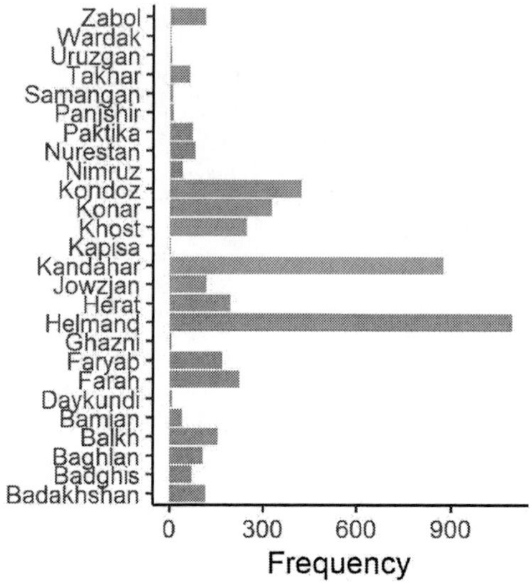

Figure 5: Provinces

2016, U.S. forces declined from 140,000 to 10,000 troops. As U.S. troops were reassigned, the number of news articles associated with this actor experience a drop from 2015 to 2016, but then it increases as the Islamic State gained traction in the region. Later on, the United States reconsidered its Afghan strategy in 2017 and increased its military presence under the new South Asia strategy. This second surge of U.S. military activity in Afghanistan reinvigorated the dynamics of conflict between 2017 and 2018.

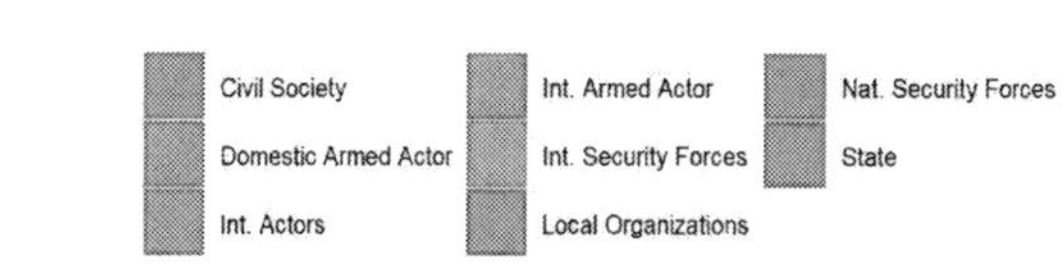

Figure 6: Temporal Trends

7. Future Research

Future research will focus on validating the coding output against manually annotated Gold Standard Records. This is will be an iterative process to improve the dictionaries of actors, actions, and locations in order to reduce the discrepancies between the computer output and the human annotation. Additional developments will consider enabling

Part of Speech tagging (POS) and Treebanks for semantic role assignment. This will help identifying of directionality of an event by defining the relationship of source-action-target. Finally, future research will enable a broader search criteria for detecting geographic locations. In its current version, Hadath only looks for a toponym (province or district) in any line containing an actor or an action. However, many instances do not mention locations in the paragraph where the event was extracted because news reports often indicate the location at the beginning of the article. In this way, future research will improve the functionality of Hadath to code event data from Arabic.

8. Conclusion

Hadath is a novel protocol for supervised event coding from text in Arabic. This software uses shallow parsing to match entries contained in dictionaries of actors, actions, and locations mentioned in a corpus written in Arabic script. In this way, Hadath contributes to research on Natural Language Processing by moving away from English-centered developments and advancing multi-lingual event data extraction. To test the functionality of Hadath in processing event data, this implementation focused on extracting events from Arabic news stories related to the conflict in Afghanistan between 2008 and 2018. To compile the collection of news articles used as corpus for this application, we developed a Machine Learning classifier to identify the specific news stories relevant to the Afghan conflict. After compiling the corpus, we used Hadath to generate event data identifying who did what to whom, when and where. The coding output allows identifying the salience of different actors related to the Afghan conflict as well as their behavioral dynamics. In this way, Hadath opens the door to future ML and NLP advances for generating event data from text written in Arabic.

9. Acknowledgements

This research was possible thanks to the support of The United States Department of Defense - Minerva Research Initiative, Award No. 71623-LS-MRI.

10. Bibliographical References

Althaus, S., Bajjalieh, J., Carter, J. F., Peyton, B., and Shalmon, D. A. (2019). Cline Center Historical Phoenix Event Data.

Arjona, A. (2016). *Rebelocracy: Social Order in the Colombian Civil War*. Cambridge University Press, NY.

Best, R. H., Carpino, C., and Crescenzi, M. J. C. (2013). An analysis of the TABARI coding system. *Conflict Management and Peace Science*, 30(4):335–348, jul.

Bond, D., Bond, J., Oh, C., Jenkins, C. J., and Taylor, C. L. (2003). Integrated Data for Events Analysis (IDEA): An Event Typology for Automated Events Data Development. *Journal of Peace Research*, 40(6):733–745.

Boschee, E., Lautenschlager, J., O'Brien, S., Shellman, S., Starz, J., and Ward, M. (2016). ICEWS Coded Event Data.

CFR. (2020). A timeline of the u.s. war in afghanistan.

Chojnacki, S., Ickler, C., Spies, M., and Wiesel, J. (2012). Event Data on Armed Conflict and Security: New Perspectives, Old Challenges, and Some Solutions. *International Interactions*, 38(4):382–401.

Gambhir, H. (2015). Isis in afghanistan. *Backgrounder, Institute for the Study of War*, 6.

Gerner, D., Schrodt, P., Yilmaz, O., and Abu-Jabr, R. (2002). The Creation of CAMEO (Conflict and Mediation Event Observations): An Event Data Framework for a Post Cold War World. In *The Annual Meeting of the American Political Science Association*. 01/10/2013.

Grimmer, J. and Steward, B. M. (2013). Text as data: The promise and pitfalls of automatic content analysis methods for political texts. *Political Analysis*, 21(3):267–297.

Halterman, A., Irvine, J., Grant, C., Jabr, K., and Yand, L. (2018). Creating and Automated Event Data System for Arabic Text.

Hammond, J. and Weidmann, N. B. (2014a). Using machine-coded event data for the micro-level study of political violence. *Research & Politics*, 1(2):2053168014539924, jul.

Hammond, J. and Weidmann, N. B. (2014b). Using machine-coded event data for the micro-level study of political violence. *Research and Politics*, 1(2):1–8.

Hollibaugh, G. E. (2018). The use of text as data methods in public administration: A review and an application to agency priorities. *Journal of Public Administration Research and Theory*, 29(3):474–490.

Hürriyetoğlu, A., Yörük, E., Yüret, D., Yoltar, Ç., Gürel, B., Duruşan, F., and Mutlu, O. (2019). A Task Set Proposal for Automatic Protest Information Collection Across Multiple Countries. In Leif Azzopardi, et al., editors, *Advances in Information Retrieval. 41st European Conference on IR Research, ECIR 2019, Cologne, Germany, April 14–18, 2019, Proceedings, Part II*. Springer.

Jhonson, S. (2011). *Where Good Ideas Come From*. Riverhead Books, New York.

Jones, S. (2008). The rise of afghanistan's insurgency: State failure and jihad. *International Security*, 32(4):7–40.

Kean, T. (2011). *The 9/11 commission report: Final report of the national commission on terrorist attacks upon the United States*. Government Printing Office.

Kenneth, K. and Thomas, C. (2017). Afghanistan: Post-taliban governance, security, and us policy. *Congressional Research Service, available at: www. fas. org/sgp/crs/row/RL30588. pdf*.

Masadykov, T., Giustozzi, A., and Page, J. M. (2010). Negotiating with the taliban: toward a solution for the afghan conflict.

Mohiuddin, S., Salam, S., Mustafa, A. M., Khan, L., Brandt, P. T., and Bhavani, T. (2016). Near Real-Time Atrocity Event Coding. *IEEE Intelligence and Security Informatics (ISI) 2016*.

O'Brien, S. (2012). A multi-method approach for near real time conflict and crisis early warning. In V. S. Subrahmanian, editor, *Handbook of Computational Approaches to Counterterrorism*, pages 401–418. Springer, NY.

Open Event Data Alliance. (2016). Universal Petrarch.

Osorio, J. and Reyes, A. (2017). Supervised event coding from text written in spanish: Introducing eventus id. *Social Science Computer Review*, 35(3):406–416.

Osorio, J., Mohamed, M., Pavon, V., and Brewer-Osorio, S. (2019a). Mapping violent presence of armed actors in colombia. *Advances of Cartography and GIScience of the International Cartographic Association*.

Osorio, J., Pavon, V., Salam, S., Holmes, J., Brandt, P. T., and Khan, L. (2019b). Translating CAMEO verbs for automated coding of event data. *International Interactions*, 45(6):1049–1064.

O'Brien, S. P. (2010). Crisis Early Warning and Decision Support: Contemporary Approaches and Thoughts on Future Research. *International Studies Review*, 12(1):87–104.

Piskorski, J., Tanev, H., Atkinson, M., Van Der Goot, E., and Zavarella, V. (2011). Online news event extraction for global crisis surveillance. In *Transactions on computational collective intelligence V*, pages 182–212. Springer.

Raleigh, C., Linke, A., Hegre, H., and Karlsen, J. (2010). Introducing acled: an armed conflict location and event dataset: special data feature. *Journal of peace research*, 47(5):651–660.

Schrodt, P. and Gerner, D. (2012). Fundamentals of Machine Coding. In *Analyzing International Event Data: A Handbook of Computer-Based Techniques*.

Schrodt, P., Gerner, D., and Yilmaz, O. (2004). Using Event Data to Monitor Contemporary Conflict in the Israeli-Palestine Dyad. In *Annual Meeting of the International Studies Association*.

Schrodt, P., Beieler, J., and Idris, M. (2014). Three's a Charm?: Open Event Data Coding with EL:DIABLO, PETRARCH, and the Open Event Data Alliance. In *International Studies Association*, Toronto.

Schrodt, P. (1998). Kansas Event Data System.

Schrodt, P. (2001). Automated Coding of International Event Data Using Sparse Parsing Techniques. Chicago. Paper presented at the annual meeting of the International Studies Association.

Schrodt, P. (2006). Twenty Years of the Kansas Event Data System Project. *The Political Methodologist*, 14(1):2–6.

Schrodt, P. (2009). TABARI. Textual Analysis by Augmented Replacement Instructions.

Schrodt, P. a. (2012). Precedents, Progress, and Prospects in Political Event Data. *International Interactions*, 38(4):546–569, sep.

Staniland, P. (2012). States, Insurgents, and Wartime Political Orders. *Perspectives on Politics*, 10(2):243–264.

Subrahmanian, V. S. (2013). *Handbook of Computational Approaches to Counterterrorism*. Springer, New York.

Sundberg, R. and Melander, E. (2013). Introducing the ucdp georeferenced event dataset. *Journal of Peace Research*, 50(4):523–532.

Wang, W., Kennedy, R., Lazer, D., and Ramakrishnan, N. (2016). Growing pains for global monitoring of societal events. *Science*, 353(6307):1502–1504.

Wilkerson, J. and Casas, A. (2017). Large-scale computerized text analysis in political science: Opportunities and challenges. *Annual Review of Political Science*, 20(1):529–544.

11. Language Resource References

Abdelali, A., Darwish, K., Durrani, N., and Mubarak, H. (2016). Farasa: A fast and furious segmenter for arabic. In *Proceedings of the 2016 Conference of the North American Chapter of the Association for Computational Linguistics: Demonstrations*, pages 11–16.

AbdelRahim Elmadany, H. M. and Magdy, W. (2018). Arsas: An arabic speech-act and sentiment corpus of tweets. In Hend Al-Khalifa, et al., editors, *Proceedings of the Eleventh International Conference on Language Resources and Evaluation (LREC 2018)*, Paris, France, May. European Language Resources Association (ELRA).

Alshutayri, A. and Atwell, E. (2018). Creating an arabic dialect text corpus by exploring twitter, facebook, and online newspapers. In Hend Al-Khalifa, et al., editors, *Proceedings of the Eleventh International Conference on Language Resources and Evaluation (LREC 2018)*, Paris, France, May. European Language Resources Association (ELRA).

Dufour, D. J. (2020). date-extractor.

Hasanain, M., Suwaileh, R., Elsayed, T., Kutlu, M., and Almerekhi, H. (2018). Evetar: building a large-scale multi-task test collection over arabic tweets. *Information Retrieval Journal*, 21(4):307–336.

Khaled Yasser, Reem Suwaileh, A. S. Y. B. M. K. and Elsayed, T. (2018). Iarabicweb16: Making a large web collection more accessible for research. In Hend Al-Khalifa, et al., editors, *Proceedings of the Eleventh International Conference on Language Resources and Evaluation (LREC 2018)*, Paris, France, may. European Language Resources Association (ELRA).

Pedregosa, F., Varoquaux, G., Gramfort, A., Michel, V., Thirion, B., Grisel, O., Blondel, M., Prettenhofer, P., Weiss, R., Dubourg, V., et al. (2011). Scikit-learn: Machine learning in python. *Journal of machine learning research*, 12(Oct):2825–2830.

Sawsan Alqahtani, M. D. and Zaghouani, W. (2018). A large scale comprehensive lexical inventory for modern standard arabic. In Hend Al-Khalifa, et al., editors, *Proceedings of the Eleventh International Conference on Language Resources and Evaluation (LREC 2018)*, Paris, France, May. European Language Resources Association (ELRA).

Suwaileh, R., Kutlu, M., Fathima, N., Elsayed, T., and Lease, M. (2016). Arabicweb16: A new crawl for today's arabic web. In *Proceedings of the 39th International ACM SIGIR conference on Research and Development in Information Retrieval*, pages 673–676.

Zaghouani, W. and Charfi, A. (2018). Guidelines and annotation framework for arabic author profiling. In Hend Al-Khalifa, et al., editors, *Proceedings of the Eleventh International Conference on Language Resources and Evaluation (LREC 2018)*, Paris, France, may. European Language Resources Association (ELRA).

Zerrouki, T. (2012). Tashaphyne, arabic light stemmer.

Proceedings of AESPEN 2020, pages 57–62
Language Resources and Evaluation Conference (LREC 2020), Marseille, 11–16 May 2020

Protest Event Analysis: A Longitudinal Analysis for Greece

Konstantina Papanikolaou[1,2], Haris Papageorgiou[1]
[1] Institute for Language and Speech Processing/Athena RC, Athens, Greece
[2] Omilia – Conversational Intelligence, Athens, Greece
kpapanikolaou@omilia.com, haris@athenarc.gr

Abstract

The advent of Big Data has shifted social science research towards computational methods. The volume of data that is nowadays available has brought a radical change in traditional approaches due to the cost and effort needed for processing. Thus, interdisciplinary approaches are necessary to cope with knowledge extraction from heterogeneous and diverse data sources. This paper presents our work in the context of protest analysis, which falls into the scope of Computational Social Science. More specifically, the contribution of this work is to describe a Computational Social Science methodology for Event Analysis. The presented methodology is generic in the sense that it can be expanded and applied in every event typology and moreover, it is innovative and suitable for interdisciplinary tasks as it incorporates the human-in-the-loop. Additionally, a case study is presented concerning Protest Analysis in Greece over the last two decades. The conceptual foundation lies mainly upon claims analysis, and newspaper data were used in order to map, document and discuss protests in Greece in a longitudinal perspective.

Keywords: Protest Event Analysis, Event Extraction

1. Introduction

Event Extraction has been a challenging task both for the field of Information Extraction in NLP and for Political and Social Sciences. As far as the latter is concerned, there have been several attempts to document events from news outlets, most of which were manual or semi-automatic.

The aim of this paper is to present an innovative computational methodology for the extraction of Protest Events from news data. Protest Event Analysis (PEA) has long been considered a significant tool for political scientists in the study of social movements and contentious politics (Wueest et al., 2013). Moving from tedious and time-consuming manual approaches used in this context, we implemented an automated methodology leveraging Natural Language Processing tools. We describe a Computational Social Science methodological approach to the research of PEA. More specifically, having Greece as reference, a longitudinal analysis of protests as a social phenomenon is documented and the impact of major socio-political events, like the recent economic crisis, is examined. Greece has been plagued by a severe financial crisis since the late 2009.

The work presented hereafter goes beyond traditional empirical approaches of social science research, thus aiming at analysing protest events using computational methods and big data analytics, exploiting a vast amount of available textual data from media outlets. We build upon an ecosystem of advanced computational content analytics technologies, capable of analysing large amounts of documents. Such topics, like PEA, are traditionally approached via small-scale, costly and non-reproducible expert coding of available political documents. However, the requirement of expert judgements is prohibitive in terms of cost and also restrictive in terms of the number of documents that could be analysed. Instead, the adopted methodology essentially develops an event database linking the major actors involved.

Therefore, a data analytics workflow was used to produce the corresponding data insights that allowed for the analysis of the complex issue of PEA and its evolution. Event analysis was performed, using news data from 2 different sources spanning the last two decades. The goal was to capture events correlated to protests along with the involved actors and record them into a large event database.

The paper is structured as follows: Related Work is discussed in Section 2. Event Extraction methodology is described in Section 3 and the Event Database in Section 4. The Evaluation of the developed system is presented in Section 5, while an Error Analysis is recorded in Section 6. Finally, the Results along with some valuable remarks are delineated in Section 7.

2. Related Work

Event extraction for political and social science has been a long-standing topic, dating back to hand coding data. Work on automatic annotation started within the KEDS/TABARI project (Shrodt et al., 1994). Evaluations have shown that hand coded and automatic coding of events show comparable performance (King and Lowe, 2003). Several coding schemes have been developed since, including the IDEA (Bond et al. 2003) and ICEWS (O' Brien 2012). One of the most renown and influential frameworks for event extraction is CAMEO (Gerner et al. 2002), which is still used by the ongoing GDELT project (Leetaru and Shrodt, 2013). All these efforts have focused on news data that have traditionally been the main source for events. Our codebook follows the same principles with a linguistically driven implementation.

Protest Events Analysis has been a central issue in the context of Political and Social sciences (Wueest et al., 2013). Despite its importance, the field of social protest in Greece is an almost uncharted territory and the related works are rather few (e.g. Kousis, 1999). Moreover, these studies are limited in their scope since they either cover a short timespan or are restricted to a specific topic (i.e. environment). This is partly due to the time-consuming nature of Protest Event Analysis (PEA), since, with a few exceptions (e.g. Imig and Tarrow, 2001, Wueest et al. 2013, Francisco n.d.), the identification and coding of protest events is done manually. The most important constraint of PEA method is the time needed for coding as the researchers have to read through literally thousands of newspaper articles and then manually record all instances of protest events. Thus, most of the projects mentioned make use of a considerable amount of resources in terms of human capital and time.

3. Event Extraction Methodology

The framework that was designed and implemented for the Event detection task, is data driven and comprises five distinct steps, namely: (a) **Events Coding**: design of a taxonomy covering a wide spectrum of protest events, (b) **Data Collection**: a significant dataset was built from several news sources, (c) **Data Exploration** where humans were involved to provide valuable insights and create targeted data collections, (d) **Data Analysis,** the main phase of the task, during which the event database was populated, (e) **Data Visualization**, an important phase of the research cycle. During this stage, the results of the Information Extraction are visualized in various ways, making them explorable, comprehensible and thus more easily interpretable. Each of the aforementioned stages is further illustrated below.

3.1 Events Coding

The first step for the Protest Events Extraction task was the knowledge representation, namely the design of a coding schema encompassing a taxonomy of protest events. This task was undertaken by social and political scientists who, in collaboration with computational scientists, developed a Codebook (Papanikolaou et al., 2016) that incorporated several event types within the broader sense of protest events along, like *Strike*, *Hunger Strike*, *Demonstration*, *Blockade* e.tc. The Codebook was based on the Political Claim Analysis (PCA) research (Stathopoulou et al., 2018), thus the analysis unit is a Claim made in the public sphere, which comprises six distinct elements: *Form*, *Actor*, *Addressee*, *Issue*, *Location*, *Time*. In Information Extraction terminology, a Claim is an Event tuple consisting of six information types, i.e.:

1. *Form* is an event type depicting a way of action, like Boycott. This is an integral part of every event instance and all the other elements are connected to it.
2. *Actor* is the entity (person or organization) that acts, performs the action.
3. *Addressee* is the entity (person or organization) that is the target of the action, to whom the action is addressed.
4. *Issue* denotes the subject matter of a protest event, namely what the protest is about.
5. *Location* is the place where a protest event took place, and,
6. *Time* depicts the time the event happened.

In order for an event to be recorded in the Event Database, the necessary elements were *Form* and one of {*Actor*, *Addressee*, *Issue*}. Moreover, the entities denoting the *Actor* or the *Addressee*, were further classified into categories representing their role or status, for example *Government*, *Asylum seekers*, *Police*, *Tertiary Trade Unions* etc. Finally, the Issue information type was categorized in pre-defined topic classes, such as *Human and Civil Rights*, *Taxation and Fiscal Policies*, *Education* etc.

Therefore, each record in the Event Database comprises of the six aforementioned constituents and their attributes. Nevertheless, it is quite common that not all of the tuple elements are completed, according to the limitations mentioned above.

3.2 Data Collection

For the Event Extraction task, a large collection of news data was used. Specifically, the dataset comprised articles published in two nationwide newspapers with different political orientation, i.e. Kathimerini, a right-oriented and Avgi, a left-oriented paper; particularly, the articles included in the Wednesday and Friday issues were collected, for the time period spanning 1996-2014. All the articles are in Greek and also metadata-like section labels, headlines and the names of the authors were gathered along with the text itself. Hence, in total 540.989 articles, 314.527 from Kathimerini and 226.462 from Avgi were collected, prepared and stored. Data preparation included tackling normalization problems and transforming the data to a human readable corpus.

3.3 Data Exploration

The phase of Data Exploration was vital to the analysis, since the followed approach is data-driven, it sets out to incorporate human-in-the-loop. Therefore, human experts explored the collected dataset using queries. The aim of this process was to determine the ways in which each event type and its constituents are expressed and lexicalized. The queries started as simple word or phrase queries and resulted in more complex ones with the use of Boolean operators. The exploration stage was also crucial for filtering the collected bulk of data and grouping them into event-oriented data clusters. This process was interactive and followed several iterations, as it was directed by the Codebook, which was also adjusted and enriched in line with the results of exploration.

One of the main goals of the Explorative Analysis was to better understand and obtain a wide view of the whole dataset. Given that the dataset consisted of two media sources reflecting ideological and idiosyncratic characteristics, it was essential to examine the different ways and linguistic means used by each news agency to report the same event. To this end, a full text search application for automated and scalable data processing was developed and used to index data and make the datasets available to the users. The core functionalities of the interface included the ability for the user to make full-text queries, simple or compound, select articles, inspect them and save the search as a new dataset to be further processed. They are also able to come back to the queries and modify them. Subsequently, in the data analysis phase, the saved queries along with the articles indicated as relevant were retrieved and stored in data clusters, one for each event type.

3.4 Data Analysis

Event Extraction is a multifaceted task (Stathopoulou et al. 2018) since several information types are involved, which need to be detected in the text and interlinked. Overall, the adopted framework was data-driven and linguistically oriented. Its foundations lay on political and social sciences, additionally incorporating human-in-the-loop. The followed workflow first detects the structural components of the event and then links them to populate the event tuples which are then recorded in the Event Database. The employed methodology is semi-supervised, in the sense that a small fraction of data was labelled and used for the system development. Additionally, it is linguistically driven, thus morphosyntactic information from basic NLP tools is utilized to identify the information types defined in the Codebook.

The general workflow for extracting events is a pipeline in the sense that every module builds over the annotations produced by previous modules (Papageorgiou and Papanikolaou, 2017). At the first step, the ILSP-NLP tools suite (Papageorgiou et al., 2002; Prokopidis et al., 2011) was leveraged for pre-processing raw text and producing annotations for Tokens, Lemmas, Chunks, Syntactic relations and Named Entities. The next module of the pipeline is the Event Analysis Unit (EAU), which takes as input the output of the pre-processing phase and at first it detects the structural elements of the event and then uses linguistic rules based on shallow syntactic patterns to link the components and create an event tuple, recording and storing it in the Event Database (Pontiki et al. 2018). The Event Extraction system is a Finite State Transducers (FSTs) cascade, implemented using Gate JAPE patterns (Cunningham et al., 2000). Figure 1 depicts the Data Analytics stack for Event Extraction:

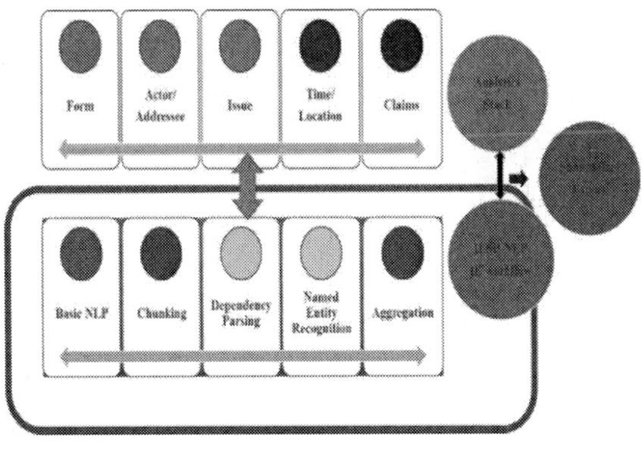

Figure 1: Data Analytics Stack

The above presented NLP workflow is fed with textual data. The basic (NLP) workflow includes segmentation (i.e. recognition of paragraph, sentence and token boundaries), part of speech tagging (i.e. assigning morphosyntactic categories to individual tokens), lemmatization (i.e. determining the base form of a token; both strike and strikes are attributed to the lemma strike), chunking (i.e. performing a shallow syntactic parsing and discovering syntactic constituents such as nominal and prepositional Phrases), parsing (i.e. determining the syntactic structure of each sentence) and Named Entity Recognition and Classification (NERC) identifying and classifying named entities into four major categories: Person, Organization, Location and Facility. This output is then forwarded to the EAU whose workflow is based on linguistic rules, given that semantics and shallow syntactic parsing patterns are exploited. EAU comprises several modules which seek to detect the structural components of the claim and to build links among them. Thus, first nominal lexicalizations of entities are identified and assigned the label *Candidate* along with Person and Organization annotations. After that, Time and Issue annotations are detected, while another module handles the identification of Forms. It is important to note that the Issue, namely the subject matter of the protest, is heavily depending on semantics. Consequently, patterns containing trigger words along with their syntactic complements were used for its detection. In such a pattern, a trigger word is "protest" and its syntactic complement a prepositional phrase starting with "about". Next, the pipeline decides whether an entity (named or nominal reference) can be assigned the label Actor or Addressee. At the final stage, the above annotations are extracted into the Event Database. The presented workflow is illustrated by the following indicative example. Given the following sentence:

The Law Society of Piraeus decided to occupy the Mortgage Registries of Piraeus and Salamis, on April 26th and 27th 2006, in protest against the serious operational problems it faces

the extracted output tuple recorded in the Database would be:

<**Actor**: *Law Society of Piraeus*, **Form**: *decided to occupy*, **Addressee**: *Mortgage Registries of Piraeus and Salamis*, **Issue**: *serious operational problems it faces*, **Time**: *April 26th and 27th 2006*, **Location**: *Piraeus, Salamis*>.

3.5 Data Visualisation

The Visualization phase is an integral part of the task as the results need to be visualized in different ways, making them understandable and easily perceivable for the human eye. That is crucial in order to be able to interpret them, find correlations or important insights and drive to conclusions according to the scope of the project.

In this context, several useful visualizations were produced from the results files. The great amount of information types that were extracted, allows for many different associations and graphs. Hence, the generated visualizations include charts, timelines, pies and word clouds. Moreover, there is the possibility to create more, filtering the results according to specific information types or attributes, configuring temporal windows or geolocating the results to produce information maps. Some of the most illustrative visualizations produced in the context of this work, are presented in the next section.

4. Event Database

The above presented methodology resulted in the population of the Event Database. More specifically, two files were created, one for each newspaper under examination, and then all the results were aggregated into one single database incorporating all the extracted event instances from both data sources. The database comprises several tables including the main information types and their attributes as were presented above. Moreover, there are tables recording metadata information. All the tables are linked using a unique ID as key.

5. Evaluation

The evaluation of our system was performed in two different ways. At first, a fraction of data was used, specifically the results of the *Strike* event type – which was the most prominent – and a time span of a month, 2/2014. The data were manually annotated, and the results compared to the system's output. The evaluation metrics used were *Precision* and *Recall*. For the selected data, Precision was 90% and Recall 93%.

Moreover, we conducted an extrinsic evaluation using data from GDELT, using event type Strike and Boycott which was part of the event coding used in our work. Since, data sources were different, the comparison was made on the basis of the recorded events in the timeline that coincided for both databases. The results can be seen in the following diagram.

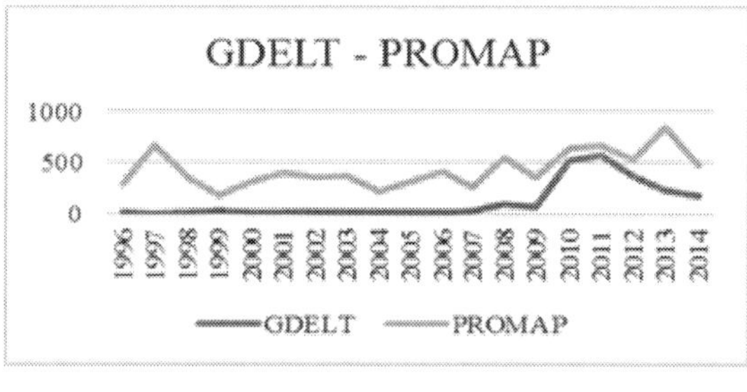

Figure 2: GDELT vs PROMAP results

6. Error Analysis

As mentioned above, the evaluation of the developed Event Analysis system showed significant results both in terms of precision and recall. Regarding recall, more experiments are needed for a more extensive evaluation, however taking into consideration the volume of the analysed data this is a quite tedious task. Despite this difficulty, at a small-scale evaluation, our system achieved a recall higher than 90% and at a large scale showed that the coverage of the events under examination is much better than GDELT, which is of great importance considering that there are no other similar analyses for Greek data. Of course, several issues arose during the process of generating the Event Database. The first and maybe obvious difficulty concerned building a common ground between people coming from different disciplines. This challenge was overcome by close and frequent interaction.

Moreover, several limitations related to Natural Language Processing resulting in errors recorded in the Database emerged. These inaccuracies appertain to three major categories. First, issues related to raw data wrangling, such as misspellings, typos as well as Optical Character Recognition (OCR) application errors during the automated conversion of raw input into machine readable text. Then, some pre-processing errors were detected, mainly related to the morphologically rich and syntactically complex nature of the Greek language. Finally, every system which automatically processes human language faces challenges associated with language complexity, like semantic ambiguity, one of the inherent characteristics of language.

7. Results - Remarks

Both quantitative and qualitative observations emerge from the analysis of the results recorded in the Protest Event Database. In an initial statistical analysis examining the total number of Claims recorded in the Event Database, we made two remarks. First, the lowest number of protest events was documented in 2004 (Fig. 3), a year of relevant economic and social prosperity when Greece drew quite a lot of attention due to the Olympic Games held in Athens, which constituted a source of national pride. Additionally, it is clear that the total number of protest events indicates an increase after 2009, when the economic crisis first ensued.

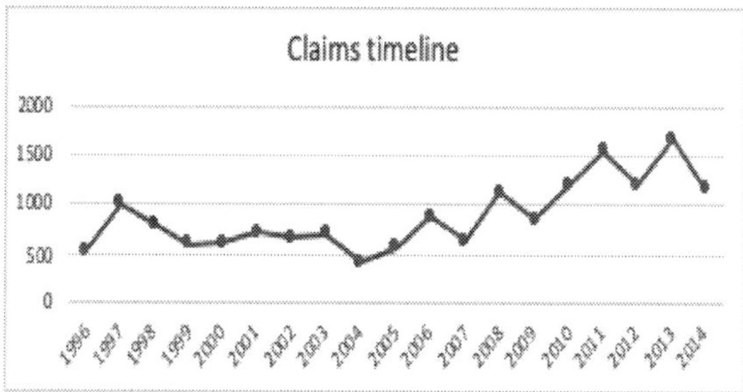

Figure 3: Total number of Claims

The top three event types in terms of frequency, were proven to be Strikes, Demonstrations and Occupations, indicating the ways the Greeks choose to protest and express their discontent (Fig. 4).

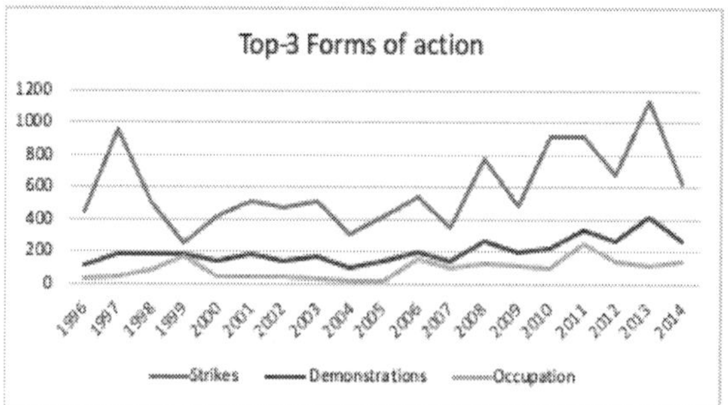

Figure 4: The top-3 forms of action

Finally, considering the most frequent topics under which the issues of the protests -taking place in the country for the examined time period- fall, it is obvious that the major concerns of the people are related to their economic status and employment affairs (Fig. 5).

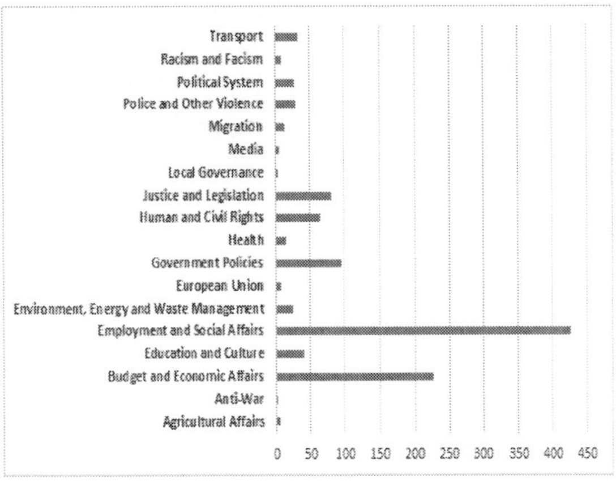

Figure 5: Issue Topic Categories

In addition, a qualitative analysis allows for some interesting observations. One of the most notable ones is the correlation between the number of recorded protest events and the election years. More specifically, looking at the chart in figure 3, we notice that the low spikes occur in election years. In particular, 1996, 2000, 2004, 2007, 2009, 2012 were all years of national elections and it is clear that the total number of protests during those years, show a significant decrease. Nevertheless, as computational scientists we can only point out a correlation, but it is designated to political scientists to interpret such phenomena (Stathopoulou et al., 2018).

8. Conclusions

In this paper, an automated approach for Protest Event Extraction was presented. In accordance with the literature relevant to Event Extraction, an innovative methodology was implemented, with one of the most prominent elements being the fact that it incorporated human-in-the-loop. Taking into consideration the fact that the work was interdisciplinary, involving both political scientists and computational experts, the exchange of knowledge was an integral part of the methodology. This was naturally an interactive process and resulted in a Codebook describing in details the expected outcome of the analysis. Several tools and technologies were then built and used for the computational implementation of the Codebook. The automatic analysis of the bulk of data collected, led to the population of a large Event Database. The development processes along with the database were described above in detail.

As an extension of the above presented work, the enrichment of the Event Database using more socio-political event categories, constitutes the future aspirations of the team. Moreover, it is our constant ambition to evolve and enhance the developed systems so as to produce the best results.

9. Acknowledgements

We acknowledge support of this work by the project “Computational Science and Technologies: Data, Content and Interaction” (MIS 5002437) which is implemented under the Action “Reinforcement of the Research and Innovation Infrastructure”, funded by the Operational Programme "Competitiveness, Entrepreneurship and Innovation" (NSRF 2014-2020) and co-financed by Greece and the European Union (European Regional Development Fund).

10. Bibliographical References

Bond, D., Bond, J., Oh, C., Jenkins, J., Taylor, C. (2003). Integrated Data for Events Analysis (IDEA): An Event Typology for automated events data development. *Journal of Peace Research,* 40(6), 733-745.

Cunningham H., Maynard D. and Tablan V. (2000). JAPE: a Java annotation patterns engine. *Research Memorandum CS–00–10*, Department of Computer Science, University of Sheffield.

Francisco, R. n.d. *European Protest and Coercion Data.* Available from: http://web.ku.edu/~ronfrand/data/. [retrieved 12 February 2016].

Gerner, D., Schrodt, P., Yilmaz, O., Abu-Jabr, R. (2002). *Conflict and Mediation Event Observations (CAMEO): a new event data framework for the analysis of foreign policy interactions.* In Annual Meeting of the International Studies Association.

Imig, D. and Tarrow, S. (eds). 2001. *Contentious Europeans Protest and Politics in an Integrating Europe.* Lanham: Rowman & Littlefield.

King, G., Lowe, W. (2003). *An automated information extraction tool for international conflict data with performance as good as human coders: a rare events evaluation design.* International Organization 57(3), 617-642.

Kousis, M. 1999. Environmental Protest Cases: The City, The Countryside, and The Grassroots in Southern Europe. In *Mobilization* 4(2): 223-238.

Leetaru, K., Shrodt, P. (2013). *GDELT: Global Data on Events, Language and Tone, 1979-2012.*

O' Brien, S. (2012). A multi-method approach for near real time conflict and crisis early warning. In Subrahmanian V. (ed) *Handbook on computational approaches to Counterterrorism.*

Papageorgiou, H. and Papanikolaou, K. (2017). Data Analytics meets Social Sciences: the Promap project. In Stathopoulou T.(ed.) *Transformations of protest in Greece.* Papazisis publishers, Athens.

Papageorgiou, H., Prokopidis, P., Demiros, I., Giouli, V., Konstantinidis, A. and Piperidis, S. (2002). Multi-level XML-based Corpus Annotation. In *Proceedings of the 3rd Language Resources and Evaluation Conference.* Las Palmas, Spain.

Papanikolaou, K., Papageorgiou, H., Papasarantopoulos, N., Stathopoulou, T., Papastefanatos, G. (2016). *"Just the Facts" with PALOMAR: Detecting Protest Events in Media Outlets and Twitter.* In International AAAI Conference on Web and Social Media. North America.

Prokopidis, P., Georgantopoulos, B. and Papageorgiou, H. (2011). A suite of NLP tools for Greek. *In Proceedings of the 10th International Conference of Greek Linguistics*, Komotini, Greece, pp. 373–383.

Shrodt, P., Shannon, D., Weddle, J. (1994). Political Science: KEDS-A Program for the Machine Coding of Event Data. In *Social Science Computer Review*.

Stathopoulou, T., Papageorgiou, H., Papanikolaou, K., Kolovou, A. (2018). Exploring the dynamics of protest with automated computational tools. A Greek case study. In *Computational Social Science in the Age of Big Data. Concepts, Methodologies, Tools, and Applications*. German Society for Online Research.

Wueest, B., Rothenhäusler, K. and Hutter, S. (2013). *Using computational linguistics to enhance protest event analysis.* Annual Conference of the Swiss Political Science Association. Zurich: University of Zurich.

Proceedings of AESPEN 2020, pages 63–68
Language Resources and Evaluation Conference (LREC 2020), Marseille, 11–16 May 2020

Event Clustering within News Articles

Faik Kerem Örs*, Süveyda Yeniterzi, Reyyan Yeniterzi***
*Sabancı University, **YAZI Information Technologies
İstanbul, Turkey
{fkerem, reyyan}@sabanciuniv.edu

Abstract

This paper summarizes our group's efforts in the event sentence coreference identification shared task, which is organized as part of the Automated Extraction of Socio-Political Events from News (AESPEN) Workshop. Our main approach consists of three steps. We initially use a transformer based model to predict whether a pair of sentences refer to the same event or not. Later, we use these predictions as the initial scores and recalculate the pair scores by considering the relation of sentences in a pair with respect to other sentences. As the last step, final scores between these sentences are used to construct the clusters, starting with the pairs with the highest scores. Our proposed approach outperforms the baseline approach across all evaluation metrics.

Keywords: Clustering, Coreference Resolution

1. Introduction

In news articles, an event can be described together with some reference to prior events or some other relevant events in order to give more background information to the reader. Therefore, news articles do not solely consist of one event throughout the article. Event sentence coreference identification (ESCI) task aims to group event containing sentences within a news article into clusters based on the event they contain. Sentences that refer to the same event belong to the same cluster while sentences that are about different events are grouped into different clusters. A good clustering of these events can improve other event related tasks like event extraction, event timeline extraction or cause and effect relation of events.

ESCI task is very similar to other coreference resolution tasks. In the entity coreference resolution task, the goal is to identify entity mentions that refer to the same entity. There is also the event coreference resolution task in which the idea is to determine which event mentions refer to the same event (Lu and Ng, 2018). Similarly, in ESCI task, the goal is to identify sentences that refer to the same event. In this particular task, the sentence as a whole is considered as an event mention.

As a result of this similarity, our proposed approach is also similar to a well-known approach in coreference resolution tasks, known as the Mention-Pair model (Ng, 2010). In this model, a binary classification model is used to classify pair of mentions as referring to either the same entity or not. After this prediction step, the pairwise prediction decisions are used to determine the coreference relations by clustering them (Ng, 2010). In our proposed approach, in addition to the prediction and clustering steps, we also use an intermediate step to re-score the pairs in order to reward consistencies and penalize inconsistencies among them.

Our proposed approach consists of three steps. We initially predict whether any given two sentences are coreferent or not. For this binary classification part, we adapt a pre-trained transformer-based neural network and fine-tune it for our task. After retrieving the predictions, we analyze how the pair of sentences interact with other sentences outside this pair. If there is an agreement on predictions, we add a reward to the score of the pair. If there is a disagreement, we decrease the score. Finally, we use a greedy approach for the clustering of sentences using their scores. Starting with the sentence pairs with the maximum scores, we construct clusters by combining more likely pairs and iterate until some stopping conditions are satisfied.

The rest of the paper is organized as following: Section 2 describes the data and the preprocessing steps, Section 3 details the proposed approach. Section 4 presents the experimental results and finally Section 5 concludes the paper with future work.

2. Data

The provided data is a subset of the data created for extracting protests from news in a cross-context setting (Hürriyetoğlu et al., 2019). The data was collected from online local English news articles from India and the news articles are about protest related events. 404 news articles, with their gold-standard labels, were provided as the training data and another 100 news articles, without any labels, are provided closer to the submission deadline for test purposes.

The data is provided in JSON format. It does not contain the whole news article, but only the sentences which contain an event. An example is provided below:


```
{"url": "http://www.newindianexpress.
   com/states/odisha/2011/apr/10/
   maoist-banners-found-243277",
 "sentences": [
   "Maoist banners found 10th April
      2011 05:14 AM KORAPUT : MAOIST
      banners were found near the
      District Primary Education
      Project (DPEP) office today in
      which the ultras threatened to
      kill Shikhya Sahayak candidates,
       outsiders to the district, who
      have been selected to join the
      service here.",
```

```
    "Maoists, in the banners, have also
        demanded release of hardcore
        cadre Ghasi who was arrested by
        police earlier this week.",
    "Similar banners were also found
        between Sunki and Ampavalli
        where Maoists also blocked road
        by felling trees."
  ],
  "sentence_no": [1, 2, 3],
  "event_clusters": [[1, 2], [3]]
}
```

As seen above, the input to the task is the sentences with provided sentence numbers, and the output is the event clusters using these sentence numbers.

2.1. Pre-processing

Data is provided in processed format, as sentences were already segmented and ready to be tokenized. After some analysis, it has been observed that in some cases, the title of the news article together with some newspaper metadata and timestamp is concatenated to the first sentence of the news article. For example, in the above example the "*Maoist banners found*" is the title which is followed by "*10th April 2011 05:14 AM KORAPUT :*". These are followed the by first sentence of the news article.
As a pre-processing step, several regular expressions are used to clean such noise from the data. After removing the title, metadata and timestamp, the remaining part has been considered as the first sentence.

3. Approach

Our proposed approach consists of three steps. In the first step, we simplify the problem by focusing on any given two sentences and predict whether they refer to the same event or not. In the next step, we use our prediction outputs (either -1 or 1) as scores and update them by analyzing not only the sentences in pairs but also their interactions with other event containing sentences in the news article. Finally, we use these scores in a greedy approach to construct the event clusters.

3.1. Same Event Prediction

In this task, all event containing sentences in a news article are grouped into pairs. Given these sentence pairs as input, the task is to predict whether these sentences refer to the same event or not. In this binary classification task, we initially convert the provided training data of news articles into sentence pairs. For the example given above, 3 sentence pairs are constructed with following labels as shown in Table 1.
As seen in Table 1, each event-containing sentence in the news article is pairwise grouped with all the rest of the event containing sentences in the news article. We specifically use the sentence numbers while creating the pairs, and use the sentence with the lower indices as the first sentence, and the one with the higher indices as the second. Therefore, for a news article with n sentences, we end up with $\frac{n(n-1)}{2}$ sentence pairs.

Pair No	First Sent. No	Second Sent. No	Label
1	1	2	TRUE
2	1	3	FALSE
3	2	3	FALSE

Table 1: Sentence Pairs and Labels for a News Article (TRUE for prediction 1 (refer to the same event) and FALSE for prediction 0 (refer to different events))

In the provided training data, on average each news article has around 4.5 sentences which contain an event. Overall, for the given 404 training instances, we end up with 4834 pairs of sentences in total. For this prediction part, we explore the pre-trained transformer-based neural network architectures. We fine-tune the following pre-trained models for our binary classification task.

- BERT (Devlin et al., 2018): Uses bidirectional transformer architecture to learn about language representation in an unsupervised manner. We fine-tune the *BERT-Large Uncased*[1] model.

- ALBERT (Lan et al., 2019): This is an efficient (**A** Lite **BERT**) version of BERT which outperformed BERT in several benchmark data sets. In this paper, we experiment with the *ALBERT-xxlarge V2*[2] model.

BERT-like models encode the provided input using different types of embeddings for tokens, segments and positions. These embeddings were initially trained on large data sets and later on fine-tuned for specific tasks. Similarly, in our case, a pair of sentences, which were separated from each other by a separator token ([SEP]), is fed into the model during the fine-tuning phase. This fine-tuned model is used for predicting whether two sentences are event coreferent or not.
BERT and ALBERT return either 0 or 1 as the prediction output. The prediction 1 is interpreted as the pair of sentences refer to the same event and 0 as they refer to different events. In order to make a better distinction between these outputs, we use -1 instead of 0 to represent the pairs which are not coreferent.

3.2. Re-scoring Sentence Pairs

As a result of the same event prediction step, all pairs have scores either 1 (when they refer to the same event) or -1 (when they refer to different events). For each pair, in addition to using this score, we also consider how this pair of sentences are in relation to other sentences. For instance, assume that two sentences s_i and s_j are predicted to be referring to the same event; therefore, they have $Score(s_i, s_j) = 1$. However, the prediction result between s_i and s_k can be same or different than the prediction result between s_j and s_k. If they are both 1, we increase the $Score(s_i, s_j)$; otherwise, if they are different, we decrease the score.

[1]https://github.com/google-research/bert
[2]https://github.com/google-research/ALBERT

The main idea here is to calculate a score for a pair sentences not just based on the pair itself but using their agreements and disagreements with other sentences as well. For any pair of sentences, s_i and s_j, among the other sentences, s_k, if there are many of them where s_i and s_j have the same prediction, then the likelihood of putting s_i and s_j to the same cluster should be higher. If the number of disagreements is higher, then the likelihood of putting s_i and s_j to the same cluster should be lower.

The proposed re-scoring algorithm is described in Algorithm 1. BERT is used to represent our fine-tuned BERT and ALBERT models. It can be replaced with any other classification model.

Algorithm 1 Re-Scoring Pairs

```
All_Scores ← []
Sentences ← sentences in the news article
for s_i in Sentences do
  for s_j in Sentences where s_j ≠ s_i do
    if BERT(s_i, s_j) = 1 then
      Score(s_i, s_j) ← 1
    else
      Score(s_i, s_j) ← −1
    end if
    for s_k in Sentences where s_k ≠ (s_i or s_j) do
      if BERT(s_i, s_k) = 1 and BERT(s_j, s_k) = 1 then
        Score(s_i, s_j) ← Score(s_i, s_j) + reward
      else if BERT(s_i, s_k) ≠ BERT(s_j, s_k) then
        Score(s_i, s_j) ← Score(s_i, s_j) − penalty
      end if
    end for
    INSERT Score(s_i, s_j) into All_Scores
  end for
end for
```

In Algorithm 1, $reward$ and $penalty$ can be set to different values between 0 and 1. The optimum values are identified using the validation data.

3.3. Constructing Event Clusters

After re-scoring the pairs, these updated scores are used to create the clusters, and for this clustering part, we use a greedy algorithm. Initially we assume that none of the sentences belongs to a cluster. Among all pairs of sentences, we only consider the ones where the score of the pair is higher than 0. For the rest, where score is 0 or less, we assume that they cannot belong to the same cluster; therefore we ignore those cases.

We sort all pairs with scores higher than 0 by their scores in descending order and, in case when there is a tie in the scores, we give priority to the sentences with lower indices. By giving that priority, we aim to start the event clustering from earlier sentences as that is how we expect the events are presented in the news articles as well. Therefore, the idea is that, in case of a tie, place the pair with the smallest sentence number before the other ones.

After sorting the pairs based on their scores and sentence indices, we begin to cluster the sentences starting with the pair with the maximum score. This merging continues until either (1) there are no more pairs of sentences left with score higher than 0, or (2) when every sentence is merged into some cluster already. In the first stopping condition, if there are any sentences left unclustered, we consider those as individual clusters. This clustering algorithm is summarized in Algorithm 2.

Our approach is similar to hierarchical clustering, as it creates clusters in a bottom-up fashion. Instead of using the minimum distance, we use the maximum score to decide the clusters.

Algorithm 2 Clustering

```
Sentences ← sentences in the news article
Groups ← group assignments for all Sentences, initially all are assigned to group 0
All_Scores ← scores retrieved from re-scoring sentence pairs
SORT (All_Scores by descending order of scores and ascending order of sentence_ids)
FILTER(All_Scores by scores > 0)
num_of_groups ← 0
for s_i, s_j in All_Scores do
  if Groups(s_i) = 0 and Groups(s_j) = 0 then
    num_of_groups ← num_of_groups + 1
    Groups(s_i) ← num_of_groups
    Groups(s_j) ← num_of_groups
  else if Groups(s_i) = 0 then
    Groups(s_i) ← Groups(s_j)
  else if Groups(s_j) = 0 then
    Groups(s_j) ← Groups(s_i)
  end if
end for
for s in Sentences do
  if Groups(s) = 0 then
    num_of_groups ← num_of_groups + 1
    Groups(s) ← num_of_groups
  end if
end for
```

Source code of the proposed three steps approach is available online[3].

3.4. An Example

In order to show how the proposed algorithms perform with respect to a single news article, an example with 7 sentences and 2 clusters, is chosen from the training data. All three steps of the approach and their respective outputs are presented in Table 2.

The first two columns represent the constructed sentence pairs. For 7 sentences we construct 21 pairs in total. Column 3 presents the outputs of the coreference classifier for these 21 pairs. The output is 1 for sentences that are coreferent and -1 for sentences that are not. These are the scores before re-scoring. Column 4 displays the scores after re-scoring. Finally, the last column shows the filtered pairs (ones with score higher than 0), the order of pairs after sorting by score and indices and, finally step by step construction of the clusters.

[3]https://github.com/su-nlp/Event-Clustering-within-News-Articles

s_i	s_j	Scores Before Re-Scoring	Scores After Re-Scoring	Orders & Clusters
2	4	1	0	-
2	27	1	2	(2) [2,27,36]
2	36	1	2	(3) [2,27,36]
2	37	-1	2	(4) [2, 27, 36, 37]
2	40	-1	-3	-
2	43	-1	-3	-
4	27	1	2	(5) [2,4,27,36,37]
4	36	1	2	(6) [2,4,27,36,37]
4	37	1	0	-
4	40	1	-2	-
4	43	1	-2	-
27	36	1	4	(1) [27,36]
27	37	1	2	(7) [2,4,27,36,37]
27	40	-1	-4	-
27	43	-1	-4	-
36	37	1	2	(8) [2,4,27,36,37]
36	40	-1	-4	-
36	43	-1	-4	-
37	40	-1	-3	-
37	43	-1	-3	-
40	43	1	2	(9) [40,43]

Table 2: An Example for Re-Scoring and Clustering (Final clusters are the same as the actual clusters, which are [2,4,27,36,37] and [40,43])

Comparing columns 3 and 4 shows the impact of re-scoring. All 21 scores have changed, either increased or decreased. Among these, the most important ones are the ones in colored cells. In these three cases, the re-scoring does not only change the score but also the sign of the score, which directly affects the final clustering. If we use the initial scores without re-scoring, than all 7 sentences will be clustered into the same cluster. However, the re-scoring step corrects the wrong prediction between pairs 4-40 and 4-43, which at the end leads sentences 40 and 43 to end up in a different cluster than the rest of the sentences. Constructing the clusters with the re-scored pairs returns the same clusters as the actual golden standard clusters.

4. Experiments

During development, we divide the provided 404 news articles into two splits (80% for training and 20% for validation). After splitting the news articles, sentence pairs are constructed for the training and validation sets. At the end, 3758 pairs of sentences are constructed for training and 1076 pairs for the validation part. During the development phase, the validation data is used to compare the performance of models. In this section, we report some experimental results over this data.

For the final phase, we received another 100 test samples from the organizers. All 404 training instances are used to train our final model to be tested on this 100 samples. Our final best model's performance over this test sample is also reported in this section.

4.1. Evaluation Metrics

The evaluation script provided by the organizers is used to evaluate the models. Adjusted Rand Index and F1 measures are reported. Since the number of sentences in the input news article has direct impact on the size of the hypothesis space and the complexity of the problem; two different averaging mechanisms are used in evaluations.

- Macro: Averaging the scores despite the number of sentences in the news article. This measure weights all news articles equally likely; therefore, it is an unweighted approach.
- Micro: This weighted metric is calculated by multiplying the score of each news article by the number of event containing sentences it contains, and then dividing the sum with total sentence count across all news articles. In other words, news articles, which contain more event containing sentences, are weighted more. As a result, more complex test cases have higher impact on the final score.

4.2. Baseline System

The baseline system developed by the organizers is two fold, which is similar to Mention-Pair models.

- As the first step, they evaluated each possible sentence pair and predicted whether they are coreferent or not. The organizers used a multi-layered perceptron model for the prediction task but the details of the model are unknown at this point.
- As the second step, they used the Correlation Clustering algorithm (Bansal et al., 2004) to process and cluster the predicted pairs from the first step.

4.3. Same Event Prediction Experiments

Before analyzing the results of the event clustering, we initially compare the performances of BERT and ALBERT on the *same event prediction* task. Results of the experiments over the validation set are presented in Table 3.

Model	Accuracy	Precision	Recall	F1
BERT	0.741	0.739	0.741	0.734
ALBERT	0.784	0.784	0.784	0.780

Table 3: Results of the Same Event Prediction Part

As seen from the Table 3, ALBERT outperforms BERT in predicting whether sentences are referring to the same event or not. Due to its better performance, we continue working with the ALBERT model in the following experiments.

4.4. Cluster Construction Experiments

In order to compare how our proposed re-scoring and cluster construction algorithms compare with respect to Correlation Clustering (CC) algorithm used in the baseline, we apply all these approaches to the prediction outputs of sentence pairs. We perform two experiments in order to analyze the individual effects of our two proposed approaches, re-scoring and clustering.

In the first experiment, we skip the re-scoring phase and directly cluster the sentences based on their initial scores from the prediction model, which are either 1 or -1. This setting is referred as *w/oRS+C*. As the second experiment, we re-score the pairs and then cluster, which is referred as *w/RS+C*. In this one, during the re-scoring part both the $reward$ and $penalty$ are set to 1. Results of these experiments on our validation data are presented in Table 4.

	ARI		F1	
	Macro	Micro	Macro	Micro
Baseline CC	0.5359	0.3964	0.6914	0.6232
Ours *w/oRS+C*	0.6231	0.5277	0.6739	0.5866
Ours *w/RS+C*	0.6088	0.5293	0.7220	0.6831

Table 4: Evaluation Results over Train/Val Splitted Data

According to the results, our proposed approach outperforms the Correlation Clustering (CC) algorithm. Using the proposed clustering algorithm standalone without the re-scoring part provides significant improvements compared to the CC algorithm in ARI metric. When the proposed clustering is combined with the re-scoring phase, drastic improvements are also observed in the F1 Measure.

In our proposed approach, the main bottleneck in terms of running time comes from the re-scoring part which has a time complexity of $O(n^3)$, where n is the number of sentences. Overall, since the number of sentences containing event is limited (on average 4.5 sentences), this running time is acceptable given the improvement in the F1 Measure.

4.5. Effect of Training Size

In the initial data set, we were provided with 404 news articles, and among those, we use 80% for the training which makes a total of 3758 pairs of sentences. Unfortunately, this is still a limited data set for fine-tuning a model. In order to see whether using a larger training set would give a higher performance, we keep everything same, except for the training set size and train different models.

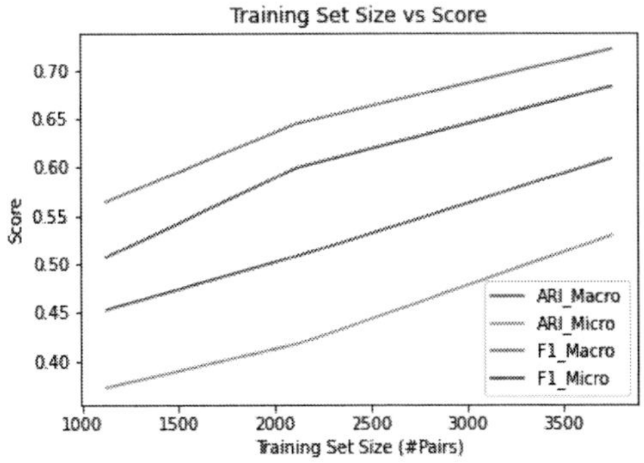

Figure 1: Performance Change with respect to Different Training Set Sizes

Testing these models on the same validation set returns the results in Figure 1. As seen from the figure, as the number of observations in training set increases, the performance consistently improves across all metrics. This indicates that even a transfered state-of-the-art pre-trained model may not be fine-tuned easily for different end-tasks. Increasing the training data would be definitely useful.

4.6. Fine-tuning $reward$ and $penalty$ Scores

In Table 4, the experiments are performed after setting both $reward$ and $penalty$ to 1. In such a case, for a pair of sentences, s_i and s_j, the *same event prediction's* result between these two sentences has the same effect as these two sentences being in agreement with other sentences. Normally agreement or disagreement with respect to other sentences may have lower effect on the final score compared to the pairwise prediction score of these sentences. Therefore, fine-tuning the values of $reward$ and $penalty$ may result in more effective re-scoring and clustering.

Values from 0.6 to 1 with an increase rate of 0.1 are used to fine-tune the $reward$ and $penalty$ scores over the validation set. Different optimum values are obtained for different metrics. Results for all 4 metrics are presented in Figure 2.

In Figure 2, the worst performance is obtained when both the $reward$ and $penalty$ is set to 1. $Penalty$ equal to 1 performs poorly for the ARI metric, and similarly $reward$ being set to 1 returns lower F1. Even though there is not a clear winner, based on the performances, both $reward$ and $penalty$ are set to 0.8 in the final model. The final results obtained with these values are presented in Table 5.

As seen from Table 5, even a slight decrease in the $reward$ and $penalty$ rates leads to an important increase in the final results.

$reward/penalty$	ARI		F1	
	Macro	Micro	Macro	Micro
1.0 / 1.0	0.6088	0.5293	0.7220	0.6831
0.8 / 0.8	0.6500	0.5749	0.7440	0.7095

Table 5: Evaluation Results with varying $reward$ and $penalty$ values with *w/RS+C* approach

4.7. Experiments on Test Set

Finally, based on our experiments over the validation set, using ALBERT together with our proposed clustering approach with $reward$ and $penalty$ set to 0.8 is our best model. Retraining this same model over the whole training data and testing it over the test data set returns the following results in Table 6. As observed, our best model consistently outperforms the baseline model across all metrics.

	ARI		F1	
	Macro	Micro	Macro	Micro
Baseline Model	0.5077	0.4064	0.5560	0.4842
Our Submission	0.6006	0.4644	0.6736	0.5898

Table 6: Evaluation Results over Test Data

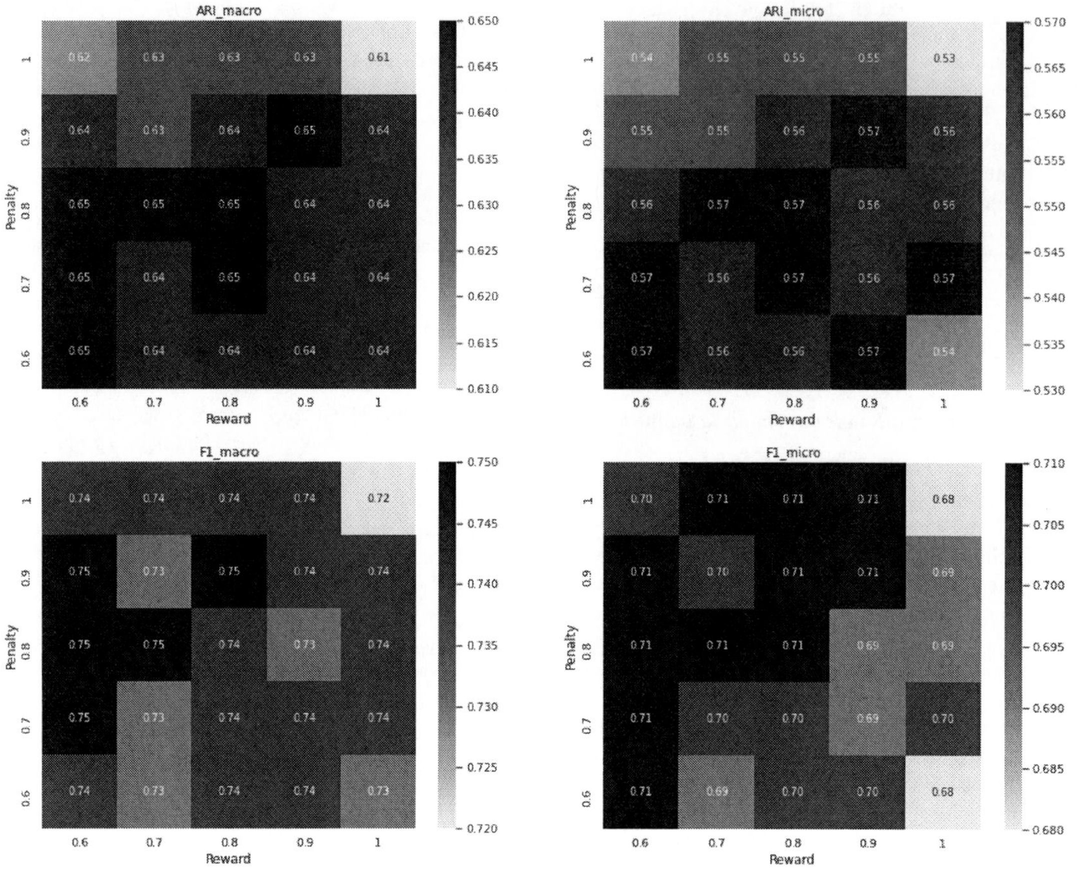

Figure 2: Performance heatmap for different values of $reward$ and $penalty$ scores

5. Conclusion

This paper summarizes our initial explorations on event sentence coreference identification within news articles. We propose a three-step approach, which is based on mention-pair model. Overall, these approaches independently and jointly work good enough to outperform the shared-task's baseline.

In future, we will perform detailed analysis of these approaches and continue improving these individual steps for our end task. An idea is to integrate the classifier's confidence levels to the scoring mechanism. Instead of using just the classification output as -1 or 1 at the initial scoring and re-scoring steps, we will analyze the effects of using classifier's confidence values directly.

6. Acknowledgements

We would like to thank to the organizers of the workshop and the shared task for organizing such an interesting challenge. We are also grateful to Dr. Ali Hürriyetoğlu for his timely and detailed responses to all of our questions during the challenge. We also thank to the anonymous reviewers for their useful and constructive feedbacks.

7. Bibliographical References

Bansal, N., Blum, A., and Chawla, S. (2004). Correlation clustering. *Machine learning*, 56(1-3):89–113.

Devlin, J., Chang, M.-W., Lee, K., and Toutanova, K. (2018). Bert: Pre-training of deep bidirectional transformers for language understanding. *arXiv preprint arXiv:1810.04805*.

Hürriyetoğlu, A., Yörük, E., Yüret, D., Yoltar, Ç., Gürel, B., Duruşan, F., Mutlu, O., and Akdemir, A. (2019). Overview of clef 2019 lab protestnews: Extracting protests from news in a cross-context setting. In Fabio Crestani, et al., editors, *Experimental IR Meets Multilinguality, Multimodality, and Interaction*, pages 425–432, Cham. Springer International Publishing.

Lan, Z., Chen, M., Goodman, S., Gimpel, K., Sharma, P., and Soricut, R. (2019). Albert: A lite bert for self-supervised learning of language representations. In *International Conference on Learning Representations*.

Lu, J. and Ng, V. (2018). Event coreference resolution: A survey of two decades of research. In *IJCAI*, pages 5479–5486.

Ng, V. (2010). Supervised noun phrase coreference research: The first fifteen years. In *Proceedings of the 48th ACL*, pages 1396–1411.